400
Quotable Quotes
From the World's
Leading
Educators

Frank Sennett

400
Quotable Quotes
From the World's
Leading
Educators

CORWIN PRESS
A Sage Publications Company
Thousand Oaks, California

For information:

Corwin Press
A Sage Publications Company
2455 Teller Road
Thousand Oaks, California 91320
www.corwinpress.com

Sage Publications Ltd.
1 Oliver's Yard
55 City Road
London EC1Y 1SP
United Kingdom

Sage Publications India Pvt. Ltd.
B-42, Panchsheel Enclave
Post Box 4109
New Delhi 110 017 India

Printed in the United States of America

Library of Congress Cataloging-in-Publication Data

400 quotable quotes from the world's leading educators /
Frank Sennett, editor.
    p. cm.
Includes index.
ISBN 0-7619-3149-X (cloth) — ISBN 0-7619-3150-3 (paper))
    1. Education—Aims and objectives—United States. 2. Educators—
Quotations. I. Sennett, Frank.
LB41.E32 2004 370'.973—dc22dc22   2003025007

This book is printed on acid-free paper.

    05 06 07 08 10 9 8 7 6 5 4 3 2

Acquisitions Editor:	Robert D. Clouse
Editorial Assistants:	Jingle Vea, Candice Ling
Production Editor:	Julia Parnell
Typesetter	C&M Digitals (P) Ltd.
Indexer:	Kathy Paparchontis
Cover Designer:	Tracy E. Miller
Production Artist:	Lisa Miller

For Nick.
Your mom and I are looking forward to meeting you.

Preface and Acknowledgments

Showcasing 400 quotations on important schooling issues from 60 seminal and influential contemporary figures in educational theory and practice, this book provides insights that will prove valuable to everyone who helps make schools tick—from teachers, librarians, and curriculum specialists to administrators, board members, and even legislators. Education students, and their instructors, will find much of value here as well.

This smorgasbord serves up bite-size food for thought to educators hungry for intellectual stimulation during their all-too-short reflection time. And by providing important new educational perspectives and fresh takes on old issues, it hopefully will inspire you to track down full-length works and other contributions by the excerpted experts. To that end, educators looking for just the right persuasive, incisive, challenging, or inspirational quotations for their speeches, proposals, and presentations can quickly and easily find just what they're looking for by using the subject index at the beginning of the book. The index groups quotations under dozens of pertinent subject headings, placing right at your fingertips a wealth of material on topics ranging from collaboration and leadership to testing and vouchers. The author index enables readers to track down excerpts by any included author, from Roland Barth to Harry Wong.

I wish to thank the staff of Gonzaga University's Foley Center Library for allowing me to raid the education stacks, as well as the fine writers whose works fill them. I also must thank my wife and family for providing encouragement and support.

Meanwhile, I extend my apologies to the great educational thinkers left out of this collection; omissions are unavoidable in such a tightly focused project, and no slights are intended. Even though some enduring educators have been left out, this collection strives to present a representative sampling of the foundational, contemporary, and popular educators of impact on the field.

This book was the brainchild of my editor at Corwin Press. When we met in 2003, he had for years been nursing the idea of a lively yet serious collection of quotations on the theory and practice of schooling restricted to top educational theorists, researchers, and leaders of the last century. He knew he'd met a kindred spirit when I described my disappointment with the education quote books typically found next to bookstore cash registers each fall—the ones featuring recycled, not-so-deep thoughts on school *daze* from such giants of pedagogy as Andy Rooney and Dave Barry. My dissatisfaction led me to edit *Teacher of the Year: More Than 400 Quotes of Insight, Inspiration, and Motivation from America's Greatest Teachers* (2002). Little did I dream my attempt to build a better educational quote book would one day lead to this wonderful new collection.

We hope you find the resulting treasury of educational wisdom enjoyable and, above all, useful in your work and intellectual life.

About the Editor

 Frank Sennett earned his fiction MFA from the University of Montana, and now teaches creative writing for UCLA Extension. He has served as editor of the K-12 journal *Curriculum Review* for nearly a decade, and has another book forthcoming from Corwin Press in 2004, titled *101 Motivational Stunts to Inspire Students*.

Subject Index

Accountability, 2, 26, 33, 66, 81, 86, 127
Administration, 5, 20, 22, 24, 30, 34, 40–41, 54, 83, 102, 104, 113–114, 117, 130
Advocacy, 54, 84
African American immersion school movement, 103
Arts, 1, 39–40, 61, 70, 85
Assessment, 14, 15–16, 20, 25, 42, 62–63, 74, 79, 83, 102, 125

Bach, Johann, 1
Brown v. Board of Education, 113
Business, 12, 49, 106, 107, 108, 115, 126

Caring, 5, 23, 34, 45, 53, 58, 98
Censorship, 18
Character education, 38, 72, 97
Charter school, 44–45, 62, 73–74
Children
    as miniature adult, 70
    at-risk, 33, 106
    authority and, 34, 45
    caring by, 5
    challenging fixed beliefs of, 17
    child development, 71
    classroom features and, 4
    curiosity of, 65

difference among, 28, 43–44, 87, 88
    discipline and, 119
    educating, as preventive investment, 31–32
    environment of, 80
    foreign language learning by, 50
    full-service school and, 75
    future and, 13, 59
    helping failing, 49
    motivating, 48
    nonutilitarian entitlements of childhood, 11–12
    opportunity to participate in society, 11
    poor, 6, 20, 43
    promoting growth of, 27
    satisfaction in teaching, 116
    taking responsibility, 57
    technology and, 91–92, 109
    testing and, 36, 66
    transitions in learning, 107–108
    unequal education and, 84
    unteachable, 116
Civic virtues, 2
Class, economic, 6–7, 20, 23, 24, 43, 54, 94, 122–123, 131

Classroom
  differentiated instruction
    in, 87
  discussion in, 14
  dynamics of, 70
  effective, 4, 10, 131
  environment of, 30
  integrated, 122–123
  legislature-centered, 67
  reassuring features of, 4
  structure in, 94
  technology in, 50
Classroom management, 31, 122
Coca-Cola, 59
Collaboration, 31, 49–50, 51, 70,
    92, 110, 111, 120, 131
Collective bargaining, 62, 66
The Color Purple, 57
Communication, 124
Community, 1, 47, 106, 107,
    125, 126
Competition, 40, 54,
    86, 118–119
Conditioning, 42
Cooperation, 12, 24, 71, 118
Creative thinking, 63, 71, 84
Creativity, 1, 9, 11, 70, 115, 123
Culture, 82
Culture of dependency, 66
Curiosity, 2
Curriculum, 24, 25, 35, 38, 52,
    67, 69, 70, 77, 78, 127

Declaration of Independence, 121
Democracy, 1, 3, 6, 7, 48, 52–53,
    64, 69, 70, 78, 105, 111, 117,
    121, 129
Dialogue, 120
Discipline, 55, 112, 119, 122
Diversity, 23, 69, 77, 92
Don Quixote, 1

Economics, 123–124
Education
  aim of, as experimental, 33
  American dream and, 106
  as conveyor belt system, 13–14
  as national priority, 51
  benefit of, 80
  challenge of, 114–115
  connection to real life, 11, 85,
    99, 105
  crisis in, 24, 124
  criticism of public, 132
  effect of, 89–90
  engaging, 36
  goal of, 9, 27
  "good," 113
  integrated, 100
  number 1 problem in, 112
  purpose of, 16
  quality, as civil right, 29
  religion and, 39
  right to, 81, 129
  "thunder analysis" of, 103
  traditional, 2, 16–17, 121, 129
  unequal, 84, 94
Educational system, as
    nonlearning system, 93
Emerson, Ralph Waldo, 97
Emotional tension, 123
Enthusiasm, 37, 83, 89, 117, 131
Environmental education, 38
Equity, 12, 29
Excellence, 5, 67, 81, 89, 98, 100

Finance, 9, 29–30, 60, 72, 79,
    81–82, 86, 106
Freedom, 52, 53, 62, 69, 94
Full-service school, 75

G.I. Bill, 83
Goethe, 50

Grades, 68, 89, 118, 130
Guilt, 45

Handel, 1
Helms, Jesse, 78
Higher education, 96
History, 23, 26–27, 36 45, 61,
    71–72, 95, 112–113, 115
Homer, 115
Human development, 71,
    59–60, 105

Identity, 26, 36, 82, 84
Illiteracy, 18, 38
Imagination, 8, 20, 33,
    34, 42, 55,
Institutional prejudice, 71–72
Integration, 20, 103, 122
Intelligence, 3, 25, 42, 45, 97,
    103, 105, 120, 130
IQ, 42, 122, 130
Isolation, 111

Jackson, Jesse, 78

Language, foreign, 50
Language development, 108
Leadership, 21, 26, 28, 33, 40, 41,
    54, 81, 87, 89, 92, 93, 104,
    108, 120, 123, 128, 131–132
Learning
    adult, 114
    as not mechanical, 55
    assessment and, 25, 83
    autonomous, 74
    breadth of, 2
    capability and, 21
    character education and, 72
    choice in, 115–116
    connection to real life, 13,
        38, 86, 111

context for teacher, 111–112
courage to teach and, 69
cultural diversity and, 92
democracy and, 6
democratic, 52–53
depth of, 47
difference in, 88
finance and, 86
foreign language, 50
"good" education and, 113
imitation and, 71
motivation for, 48
organization metaphor
    and, 32
performance-based, 119
personalization and, 56
politics and, 70
positive thinking and, 22
principal and, 120
prior knowledge and, 46
process of, 97
psychology and, 21–22
relationship to democracy, 129
relationship with teaching, 73
service learning, 98
teacher preparation
    and, 96
technology and, 65
testing and, 114
thinking and, 8
through understanding, 42
vision and, 23
Liberal education, 102
Liberty, 35, 53, 121
Lincoln, Abraham, 132
Literacy, 19, 57–58, 88, 96
Loads, teaching, 15
Locke, John, 127

Management, 7–8, 75, 92, 122
Mandates, 24, 71, 75

Mathematics, 3, 18, 41, 81, 82, 86, 121
Maugham, Somerset, 123
McDonald's, 82
Mentors, 19, 111, 117
Mission, 3, 44, 73, 92, 105, 121
Mistrust/trust, 12, 22, 30, 35, 127
Moby Dick, 57
Morality, 11, 90, 97, 100, 102, 113, 118, 119
Motivation, 10, 48, 51, 103, 121, 126
MTV, 92

Nietzsche, Friedrich, 13

Ownership, 87

Parents, 1, 6, 12, 13, 14, 32, 34, 41, 43, 54, 57, 64, 69, 75–76, 83, 95, 114, 118, 130
Philanthropies, 78
Plessy v. Ferguson, 113
Poetry, 96, 115
Politics, 6–7, 30, 48, 54, 60, 64, 66–67, 70, 75, 78, 86, 98, 99–100, 107, 117, 132
Power, 2–3, 6, 8–9, 23, 27, 36, 39, 48, 61, 62, 77, 93, 108, 117, 126, 131–132
Preparation, 46–47, 77, 96
Preschool/kindergarten, 67, 128
Principal, 21, 62, 81, 91, 93, 106, 110–111, 117, 120, 128, 141
Private schools, 39, 44, 69
Privatization, 67
Problem solving, 63
Productivity, 98, 118–119
Professional, teacher as, 20, 68, 73, 76

Professional development, 3, 40, 58, 92, 102
Public schools, 5, 6–7, 44, 57–58, 69, 84, 100–101, 124, 129–130

Quality, 2, 20, 25, 30, 49, 60, 77, 82, 85, 93, 97, 98, 105, 108, 109, 117, 129, 130

Race, 22, 112–113, 114
Reading, 3, 8–9, 18–19, 50, 56–57, 81, 82, 90, 107–108, 119, 121, 125, 128
Reflection, 4, 65, 107
Reform
    as school-by-school process, 25
    choice in, 117
    creating climate for, 37
    finance and, 78, 81–82, 86
    focus of, 17
    full-service school and, 75
    genuine, 125
    importance of, 45
    institutional, 132
    leadership and, 123
    loose foundation of, 46
    need for clarity in, 41
    need for multiple, 47
    parents and, 32
    purpose of school and, 100
    standards and, 2, 9, 125
    support for, 21, 28
    test scores and, 12
    unrealistic assumptions and, 86
Religion, 39, 115
Research, 18, 19, 20, 32, 35, 40, 46, 49, 60, 76, 91

Respect, 9–10, 15, 28, 53, 58, 83, 89, 127
Responsibility, 51, 53, 57, 68, 75, 77, 80, 81, 85, 97, 99, 100, 118–119, 121, 122

Salaries, 2–3, 29–30, 49, 52, 101, 102
Scarlatti, Domenico, 1
School choice, 43–44, 44, 59, 86
Schools
  as refuge, 107
  blaming, 93
  charter, 44–45, 62, 73–74
  effective, 56, 89
  evaluating through observation, 105–106
  full-service, 75
  future of society and, 13
  improvement in, 16, 89
  inadequacy of, 37–38
  judging, 77
  private, 39, 44, 69
  public, 5, 6–7, 44, 57–58, 69, 84, 100–101, 129–130
  traditional, 20
Science, 1, 18, 38–39, 47, 58, 86, 105, 122
Self-esteem movement, 126
Service learning, 98
Shakespeare, William, 1
Silas Marner, 57
Slogans, 86, 87
Spirituality, 40
Sportsmanship, 70
Standards, 2, 6, 9, 23, 24, 26, 29, 37, 49, 58, 63, 71, 79, 102, 112, 118, 124, 125, 130
Structure, 52

Studies, hierarchy of, 104
Success, 7–8

Teacher
  as role model, 53
  availability to student, 15
  basics/complexities, 3–4
  common purpose with administrator, 104
  educating, 126
  effective/good, 2–3, 19, 55, 57, 122
  further education of, 119
  getting to know student, 14
  improving performance of, 93
  influence on student, 14–15
  learning context for, 111–112
  misassignment of, 120
  motivating, 10
  need for support among, 110
  never-ending job of, 95
  new, 91, 130
  quality vs. quantity of, 109
  relationship with administrator, 14, 34, 104, 128
  self-reflection, 107, 110
  teacher culture, 26, 64–65
  teacher shortage, 68
  teaching loads, 15
  training of, 111
Teaching
  artistry of, 5, 34, 102, 127
  as demanding, 110
  as empowerment, 42
  as knowing, 27
  as not scientific, 35
  assessment and, 25
  "bright person myth" of, 96
  courage and, 68–69

democracy and, 6
effective, 81
goals in, 5
good, 17, 29, 36
highlight of, 121
importance of student in, 106
interdisciplinary, 119
knowledge and, 90
learning and, 73
listening and, 70
loneliness of, 109
nature of, 46
organization metaphor
    and, 32
personalization and, 56
preparation for, 46–47, 77, 96
realm of, 63–64
reason for, 98
satisfaction in, 116
student effort and, 72
vs. standardized testing, 94
Teaching style
art of instruction, 76
breadth of, 42
dialogue, 41, 80
differentiated instruction, 87
for at-risk child, 33
getting interest, 59
personalization, 56
progressive, 16–17
question-oriented, 56
real-world application, 52
teaching what interests you,
    9–10
Technology, 2, 20, 51, 65, 91–92,
    109, 131
Testing
accountability and, 26, 66, 127
annual, 116
as artificial, 99, 124–125
as mechanized, 114

challenging test, 130
concentration on scores, 95
core goals of schooling and, 2
creativity and, 10–11
enthusiasm for, 117
intelligence and, 103, 105
IQ test, 42, 122
job performance and, 12
long term projects and, 20
low test scores, 85–86
multiple-choice, 29, 31
preparing for, 122
public officials and, 36
reading scores, 118–119
responsibility and, 97
standardized, 26, 53, 88, 94,
    113–114
time spent on, 79
Theory of schoolhouse, 74–75
Thinking
conversation and, 8
correct, 49
higher-order, 17, 111
independent, 26–27
nature of, 103
psychology and, 21–22
Trust/mistrust, 12, 22, 30, 35, 127
Truth, 7, 16, 52–53, 74, 117

Uniformity, 24, 55, 77, 94
Unions, 101, 104

Ventura, Jesse, 78
Violence, 15, 36, 72
Vision, 23, 61, 75, 92, 95, 104,
    120, 123, 125, 131–132
Vouchers, 43, 44–45, 83

Workers, 11, 12, 34, 118
Writing, 3, 12, 38, 81, 111, 121,
    125, 128

Educating America

What the best and wisest parent wants for his own child, that must the community want for all of its children. Any other ideal for our schools is narrow and unlovely; acted upon, it destroys our democracy.

—John Dewey (1859-1952), Author
Democracy and Education

The dawn of centuries has always been a good time to explore creativity. In 1601, for example, Shakespeare's sonnets were published, Cervantes' Don Quixote went to print, and Bach, Handel and Domenico Scarlatti were born. Within the first few years of the past century we had the discovery of the electron, heavier than air flight, the discovery of X-rays, and numerous other developments in the sciences and arts. There is no reason to think that the coming years will be any less exciting than those clustered around the start of other centuries. If anything, the next few years will be even more thrilling.

—David Thornburg, Founder
The Thornburg Center

1

Education is about learning to deal with uncertainty and ambiguity. It is about learning to savor the quality of the journey. It is about inquiry and deliberation. It is about becoming critically minded and intellectually curious, and it is about learning how to frame and pursue your own educational aims.

—Elliot W. Eisner, Stanford University

What we need to talk about openly in debates about schooling is not whether a traditional school is better or worse than a progressive school but whether each cultivates civic virtues. Current talk about standards-based reform, test scores, more technology, and accountability is not about this core goal of schooling.

—Larry Cuban, Stanford University

School is not a place for important people who do not need to learn and unimportant people who do. Instead, school is a place where students discover, and adults rediscover, the joys, the difficulties, and the satisfactions of learning.

—Roland S. Barth, Founder
Harvard Principal Center

Powerful people take the jobs that entrust them with the important things. If you want good people in the teaching profession, you have to set it up so teachers have authority over the important things. . . . Listen to the good teachers. They talk about pay, yes.

But they talk more passionately about the fact that other people are telling them what to do. I would say the heart of the matter is substantial control over time and materials; pay follows that.

—Theodore R. Sizer, Founder
Coalition of Essential Schools

Public education's ostensible mission, the development of an intelligent populace and a popular intelligence, requires that all individuals have access to education that prepares them to debate and decide among competing ideas, to weigh the individual and the common good, and to make judgments that sustain democratic institutions and ideals.

—Linda Darling-Hammond
Stanford University

There is a much more sensible approach to improving education; in fact, I believe it is the only approach likely to be effective in the long run. That is to produce a cohort of teachers who believe they are professionals, who act like professionals, and who are treated as professionals.

—Howard Gardner
Harvard University

Evidence is mounting to suggest that the school's limitations are much less severe in teaching the fundamentals of reading, writing, and figuring—the so-called basics—than in teaching more complex

abilities. We live in an era of rapidly expanding opportunities to acquire information but of constricting opportunities to reflect, engage in sustained discourse with others, and clarify our beliefs about the times and circumstances in which we live. If our schools need improvements in the basics, they need—perhaps more—a fresh examination of their role in a society undergoing rapid change.

—John I. Goodlad
Center for Educational Renewal
University of Washington

The features of our children's classrooms that we find the most reassuring—largely because we recognize them from our own days in school—typically turn out to be those least likely to help students become effective and enthusiastic learners.

—Alfie Kohn, educational theorist

I like to think of a good classroom as a kind of ménage à trois *in which there is the teacher, the student, and the subject matter. The teacher loves both the subject and the student, and the kind of love that really makes learning happen is where you try to introduce two things you love to one another. In a sense you introduce them and get yourself out of the way so they can forge a relationship of their own.*

—Parker J. Palmer, Founder, Fetzer
Institute Teacher Formation Program

It is often asserted that public schools are change resistant. This is not so. There is in fact so much change occurring in schools that teachers and school administrators rightly feel overwhelmed by it. However, this change is seldom accompanied by clear improvements in performance. Schools are change prone, but they are also change inept.

—Phillip C. Schlechty, Founder, Center
for Leadership in School Reform

All children must learn to care for other human beings, and all must find an ultimate concern in some center of care: care for self, for intimate others, for associates and acquaintances, for distant others, for animals, for plants and the physical environment, for objects and instruments, and for ideas. Within each of these centers, we can find many themes on which to build courses, topical seminars, projects, reading lists, and dialogue.

—Nel Noddings, Stanford University

No doubt some excellent educational work is being done by artistic teachers who do not have a clear conception of goals but do have an intuitive sense of what is good teaching, what materials are significant, what topics are worth dealing with and how to present material and develop topics effectively with students. Nevertheless, if an educational program is to be planned and if efforts for continued improvement are to be made, it is very necessary to have some conception of the goals that are being aimed at.

—Ralph W. Tyler (1902-1994), Author
*Basic Principles of Curriculum and
Instruction*

Poor children get off to a bad start before they're born. Their mothers are likely to get prenatal care late, if at all, which can impair later intellectual functioning. They are more than three times as likely as nonpoor children to have stunted growth. They are about twice as likely to have physical and mental disabilities, and are seven times more likely to be abused or neglected. And they are more than three times more likely to die. What these kids need are high standards, right?

—Gerald W. Bracey
educational researcher

We must realize that the basic goal of our schools is to prepare students to engage productively in a democracy. We must organize and operate our own schools in accord with the democratic principles of our society. Teaching and learning between students and teachers must demonstrate, in actions, the relationship between education and democracy—the power of learning for engagement in real issues.

—Carl D. Glickman, Founder
The Program for School Improvement

We talk of the importance of "public schools in a democracy," yet we know that our "public" schools today are profoundly segregated by class—the wealthy suburbs and the inner city. The contrast between the Lake Forests and the Chicagos, the Scarsdales and the Harlems, is blatant. We all know this, but we mention it as rarely as possible. To achieve a "melting pot"—if that is what Americans want—will require more political will than most can contemplate. And if Americans in

fact do not want a "melting pot," we dare not bluntly admit that fact.

—Theodore R. Sizer, Founder
Coalition of Essential Schools

Because they don't teach the truth about the world, schools have to rely on beating students over the head with propaganda about democracy. If schools were, in reality, democratic, there would be no need to bombard students with platitudes about democracy. They would simply act and behave democratically, and we know that does not happen. The more there is a need to talk about the ideals of democracy, the less democratic the system usually is.

—Noam Chomsky, Massachusetts
Institute of Technology

It is largely through the crucial role it plays in individual and collective transactions between employers (who wish to secure the skills ensured by a title at the lowest cost) and employees (who intend to assert the rights inscribed in their diplomas) that the educational system directly contributes to the reproduction of social classifications.

—Pierre Bourdieu (1930-2002)
Author, *Homo Academicus*

The emphasis on school-based management over the past decade has led us down the garden path. Success can only happen at the

school level, but it also is unlikely to happen on any scale, and cannot be sustained if the infrastructure is not dramatically strengthened.

> —Michael Fullan, Ontario Institute
> for Studies in Education
> University of Toronto

Learning is more than the acquisition of the ability to think; it is the acquisition of many specialized abilities for thinking about a variety of things

> —L.S. Vygotsky (1896-1934), Author
> *Thought and Language*

We need to provide opportunities for youngsters and adolescents to engage in challenging kinds of conversation, and we need to help them learn how to do so. Such conversation is all too rare in schools. I use "conversation" seriously, for challenging conversation is an intellectual affair. It has to do with thinking about what people have said and responding reflectively, analytically, and imaginatively to that process. The practice of conversation is almost a lost art. We turn to talk shows to experience what we cannot do very well or very often.

> —Elliot W. Eisner, Stanford University

I define reading as a message-getting, problem-solving activity which increases in power and flexibility the more it is

*practiced. . . . As we progress along the lines of a text it is not
unlike the process of finding footholds when climbing up
a cliff-face, yet the achievement is in the single completed task.*

—Marie M. Clay, Founder
Reading Recovery

*The principal goal of education in the schools should be creating
men and women who are capable of doing new things, not simply
repeating what other generations have done; men and women who
are creative, inventive and discoverers, who can be critical and
verify, and not accept, everything they are offered.*

—Jean Piaget (1896-1980), Author
The Origins of Intelligence in Children

*Standards-based education requires schools literally to double or
triple education results—i.e., student achievement. Since there is
little if any hope that funding will double or triple, accomplishing
the goals of standards-based education reform will require schools
to use resources more productively and to reallocate resources to
new and more effective education strategies.*

—Allan Odden
University of Wisconsin

*We gain our interests mostly from picking up on the interests of
people we care for and respect: Don't worry about what you should
teach as much as what you want to teach. As long as they remember*

*you, they will have learned information that you value as a
professional and they will have profited from being in your classes.*

—William Glasser, Founder
The William Glasser Institute

*The first days of school can make or break you. Based on what a
teacher does or does not do, a teacher will either have or not have
an effective classroom for the rest of the year. What happens on the
first days of school will be an accurate indicator of your success for
the rest of the school year.*

—Harry and Rosemary Wong
educational consultants

*Teachers, for the most part, enter teaching because they love the
work and think they can do it well. Many encounter places that
don't support their best work. The best way to motivate them is to
create schools that are lively and well-supplied, exciting places to
be, where people can do their work, where they are not interrupted
by foolish announcements on the P.A., where they are given the
support they need to work with children with special needs. Leave
the carrots and sticks out of it.*

—Susan Moore Johnson
Harvard University

*The name of the test varies, but the fact of some test or another
doesn't. The teacher is trying desperately to get through a lesson; it*

is going slower than it was supposed to because lessons hardly ever go exactly the way they are planned. . . . Then a student suggests a way of making a lesson that is going too slowly go even more slowly. The teacher's instantaneous reflex is to shoot a bullet— right through the student's idea, but also through the student's desire to be creative.

—Robert J. Sternberg, Yale University

We do not extend help to children solely because of moral obligations. It is also because we have faith in the future of our society, in its progress, its values, and its traditions, and we want our children to have every possible opportunity to participate in the society and contribute to it.

—Marian Wright Edelman, Founder
Children's Defense Fund

Life is more than meat, even though life without food dies. Living is not for earning, earning is for living. The man that spends his life earning a living, has never lived. The education that trains men simply for earning a living is not education.

—W.E.B. Du Bois (1868-1963), Author
The Souls of Black Folk

Childhood ought to have at least a few entitlements that aren't entangled with utilitarian considerations. One of them should be the right to a degree of unencumbered satisfaction

in the sheer delight and goodness of existence in itself. Another ought to be the confidence of knowing that one's presence on this earth is taken as an unconditioned blessing that is not contaminated by the economic uses that a nation does or does not have for you.

—Jonathan Kozol
educational researcher

Some education reformers claim that test scores bear on job performance and that higher student scores today will translate into better adult workers tomorrow. But the evidence doesn't support this contention. Indeed, if employers come to believe that test scores are important and start selecting new hires based on the scores alone, it could have a detrimental impact on both the efficiency and equity of their businesses.

—Gerald W. Bracey
educational researcher

Listen to what employers ask of educators and parents in new hires for entry-level jobs. Again and again, they say that they want recent high school and college graduates who can be trusted, care about the work they do, finish tasks, are self-starters, show initiative, can define problems, write and think clearly and work cooperatively. Not a word about how to use databases, manage spreadsheets or do PowerPoint presentations.

—Larry Cuban, Stanford University

For school to make sense, the young, their parents, and their teachers must have a god to serve, or, even better, several gods. If they have none, school is pointless. Nietzsche's famous aphorism is relevant here: "He who has a why to live can bear with almost any how." This applies as much to learning as to living. To put it simply, there is no surer way to bring an end to schooling than for it to have no end.

—Neil Postman (1931–2003), Author
Teaching as a Subversive Activity

Children may be 20 percent of the population, but they are 100 percent of the future.

—David B. Tyack, Stanford University

As a society becomes more enlightened, it realizes that it is responsible not to transmit and conserve the whole of its existing achievements, but only such as make for a better future society. The school is its chief agency for the accomplishment of this end.

—John Dewey (1859-1952), Author
Democracy and Education

Students move along a conveyor belt from one teacher to the next, grade to grade, and class period to class period to be stamped with lessons before they move on. They have little opportunity to become

well known over a sustained period of time to any adults who can consider them as whole people or as developing intellects.

—Linda Darling-Hammond
Stanford University

At the bottom line teachers, of necessity, look after their own best interests and those of their pupils. Ultimately no one else will. Principals look after the best interests of all the children, all the teachers, and all the parents—and themselves. In the end no one else will. Unfortunately, in attempting to fulfill their responsibilities and protect themselves, teachers and principals have demonstrated a unique capacity to inflict cruel and unusual punishment on one another.

—Roland S. Barth, Founder
Harvard Principal Center

A teacher who understands the need for teaching and learning to be a good match for students looks for every opportunity to know her students better. She sees conversations with individuals, classroom discussions, student work, observation, and formal assessment as a way to gather just a little more insight about what works for each learner.

—Carol Ann Tomlinson
University of Virginia

Classroom teachers give young people what they sometimes get nowhere else in society—a sense that they have promise, that they

have talents, that they are special. If you're a young person who is not quite sure that you are welcome in this society, one of the most important people in your life could be a teacher who accepts you.

—Parker J. Palmer, Founder, Fetzer
Institute Teacher Formation Program

Being known signals a kind of respect: You're 14, you may be a ragamuffin or worse, but you still deserve respect. If schools are to deal with violence, the per-teacher loads have to be reduced dramatically; the schools have to be places where the kids are unequivocally known.

—Theodore R. Sizer, Founder
Coalition of Essential Schools

What I must do is to be totally and nonselectively present to the student—to each student—as he addresses me. The time interval may be brief but the encounter is total.

—Nel Noddings, Stanford University

The really important dependent variables in education are not located in classrooms. Nor are they located in schools. The really important dependent variables are located outside schools. Our assessment practices haven't even begun to scratch that surface. It's what students do with what they learn when they

can do what they want to do that is the real measure of educational achievement.

—Elliot W. Eisner, Stanford University

I see the purpose of education as helping people understand the best answers that cultures and societies have come up with to basic questions, what I would call essential questions. So at the end we can form our own personal answers to those questions, which will be based to a significant extent on how other people have approached them, and will at the same time allow us to make our own syntheses.

—Howard Gardner
Harvard University

Most efforts to improve schools founder on reefs of ignorance—ignorance of the ways schools function in general and ignorance of the inner workings of selected schools in particular.

—John I. Goodlad, Center for
Educational Renewal, University
of Washington

To those of us who spend time in real schools . . . claims about the dominance of progressive teaching represent an inversion of the truth so audacious as to be downright comical. As we slip into a new century, traditional education is alive and well and—as I see

it—damaging a whole new generation of students. If this isn't always obvious, it may be because we rarely think about how many aspects of education could be different but aren't.

—Alfie Kohn, educational theorist

Change leaders, funding agencies, and policy makers too often overlook or look past creating in school systems conditions that are supportive of change and instead fasten on programs and projects that promise to have immediate results. In a word, efforts to improve schools usually attend more to the introduction of projects and programs than to the systems in which these programs and projects are to be implemented.

—Phillip C. Schlechty, Founder
Center for Leadership
in School Reform

A large part of what we call "good teaching" is the teacher's ability to attain affective objectives through challenging the students' fixed beliefs. . . . A child is not truly using his higher order thinking skills until he no longer believes in absolutes of right and wrong.

—Benjamin S. Bloom (1913-1999)
Author, *Taxonomy*
of Educational Objectives

Even if illiteracy does not wipe out the socially created
relationships between language, thought, and reality,
it is a handicap that becomes an obstacle to achieving full
citizenship.

—Paulo Freire (1921-1997), Author
Pedagogy of the Oppressed

There is no censorship so perfect, so complete as that imposed on
the nonreader.

—Jonathan Kozol
educational researcher

Reading is the foundation of education. If you are a poor
reader then your math or science or any other textbook might as
well be a fire hydrant for all the good it does. So it is critical that
children learn this important skill as soon as they enter school.
It is also vital that children with difficulties learning to read
get help right away, because research tells us that those who
are not good readers by third grade have almost no chance of
catching up.

—Rod Paige
U.S. Secretary of Education

When we are reading about learning to read we can always check
what authorities are claiming against what we are able to observe
in our own behavior as readers. It is helpful to use this resource as

*one way of checking whether some claim about literacy learning
makes sense to you.*

—Marie M. Clay, Founder
Reading Recovery

*It is my belief that the thing which we should cultivate in our
teachers is more the* spirit *than the mechanical skill of the scientist.*

—Maria Montessori (1870-1952)
Author, *The Montessori Method*

*What is desired is that the teacher cease being a lecturer, satisfied
with transmitting ready-made solutions; his role should rather be
that of a mentor stimulating initiative and research.*

—Jean Piaget (1896-1980), Author
The Origins of Intelligence in Children

*Mentors and apprentices are partners in an ancient human dance,
and one of teaching's great rewards is the daily chance it gives us to
get back on the dance floor. It is the dance of the spiraling
generations, in which the old empower the young with their
experience and the young empower the old with new life, reweaving
the fabric of the human community as they touch and turn.*

—Parker J. Palmer, Founder, Fetzer
Institute Teacher Formation Program

I do not disagree with those who argue that achievement levels can be raised without integration. Certainly, the research shows that it is possible to raise the achievement of poor children. But that is not the point. Even as we continue to work to raise the achievement scores of these children, we must remember that high achievement alone does not complete the equation for quality education. A fundamental element would still be lacking. . . . Our children would not be profiting from the opportunity to learn and grow together.

—Gerald N. Tirozzi, Executive
Director, National Association of
Secondary School Principals

We should broaden our concept of testing to include assessments based on long-term interdisciplinary projects—in other words, on something bearing a resemblance to reality. Then technology will have a truly creative, constructive role to play.

—David Thornburg, Founder
The Thornburg Center

As traditional schools operate now, teachers are not treated as professionals. Everyone, administrators, school boards, state departments, and the legislature, and the governors' offices, has a hand in telling teachers what they want done, how to do it, and how it will be measured. There is no job that requires professionals more than teaching, yet there is no job in which the people who do it are treated in ways that make it impossible for them to be professional. Imagine what medicine or law would be like if physicians and lawyers were treated as teachers are.

—William Glasser, Founder
The William Glasser Institute

Very few school leaders know how important it is to learn how to facilitate your opposition. Why? Because otherwise, they agree to your face and then subvert you when you're not looking.

—Lee G. Bolman, University of
Missouri at Kansas City; and
Terrence E. Deal, University of
Southern California

No reform can succeed without the endorsement and energetic support of teachers and principals, who must not only change as educators but make change happen in their schools. The heady times of school reform have made these people cautious about sure-fire solutions and skeptical of outsiders who claim they have the answers.

—Susan Moore Johnson
Harvard University

In regard to the growth of the mind, we should set our goals very, very high, because we know that most people are capable of more than they do or are.

—Seymour B. Sarason, Yale University

Psychology should be the chief basic science upon which the practices of education depend. It should have supplied education with the information it needs concerning the processes of understanding, learning, and thinking, among other things. One of the difficulties has been that such theory as has been developed has been based primarily upon studies of behavior of rats and pigeons.

As someone has said, some of the theory thus developed has been an insult even to the rat.

—J.P. Guilford (1897-1988), Author
The Nature of Human Intelligence

When we haven't been smart enough to figure out how to study something, we'll often say that it can't be studied. What we should say is, "Well, I haven't figured that out yet—but there's always next week."

—Robert J. Sternberg, Yale University

I have developed a virtually total distrust of any numbers coming out of school bureaucracies; the majority are likely to be sheer fiction.

—Theodore R. Sizer, Founder
Coalition of Essential Schools

To prepare teachers to be successful with African American students, teacher educators must help prospective teachers recognize the ways that race and racism structure the everyday experiences of all Americans. More specifically, teachers must understand how race and racism negatively impact African American students and their ability to successfully negotiate schools and classrooms.

—Gloria Ladson-Billings, University
of Wisconsin

When people truly share a vision they are connected, bound together by a common aspiration. Personal visions derive their power from an individual's deep caring for the vision. Shared visions derive their power from a common caring. In fact, we have come to believe that one of the reasons people seek to build shared visions is their desire to be connected in an important undertaking. Shared vision is vital for the learning organization because it provides the focus and energy for learning.

—Peter M. Senge, Massachusetts
Institute of Technology

Obviously a society to which stratification into separate classes would be fatal, must see to it that intellectual opportunities are accessible to all on equable and easy terms. A society marked off into classes need be specially attentive only to the education of its ruling elements. A society which is mobile, which is full of channels for the distribution of a change occurring anywhere, must see to it that its members are educated to personal initiative and adaptability. Otherwise, they will be overwhelmed by the changes in which they are caught and whose significance or connections they do not perceive.

—John Dewey (1859-1952), Author
Democracy and Education

America is the most diverse country in the history of world. How are we dealing with diversity in schools? Standardization!

—Paul D. Houston, Executive Director
American Association of School
Administrators

[A] potential consequence of this movement toward curricular uniformity and instructional standardization is the silent, pervasive spread of fatigue and cynicism among teachers and administrators. Hundreds of objectives, detailed lesson plans, numerous tests, and much recordkeeping persuades some teachers that they are more clerks than schoolmasters. If anything, state curricular mandates . . . threaten to deskill teaching.

—Larry Cuban
Stanford University

The relationships among adults in schools are the basis, the precondition, the sine qua non *that allow, energize, and sustain all other attempts at school improvement. Unless adults talk with one another, observe one another, and help one another, very little will change.*

—Roland S. Barth, Founder
Harvard Principal Center

If all U.S. schools could function as well as the most advantaged do, there would be no need for systemic change. It is not that U.S. teachers and students cannot succeed when they are well supported, it is that the system fails to support so many of them. This is the real crisis of American education.

—Linda Darling-Hammond
Stanford University

Performance assessment affords us, in principle, an opportunity to develop ways of revealing the distinctive features of individual students. It affords us an opportunity to secure information about learning that can help improve the quality of both curriculum and teaching. In short, it affords us an opportunity to use evaluation formatively and to treat assessment as an educational medium. But it is unlikely that such opportunities will be realized if the public's attitudes and expectations toward schooling are not changed, and it is unlikely that they will change without revision of the policies that affect the educational and social mobility of students in schools.

—Elliot W. Eisner, Stanford University

I remain skeptical that there is such a thing as pure intelligence. In my view, what we count as intelligence changes from one era to another—the intelligence needed to succeed in an agricultural society may be different from that needed to thrive in a computer-based society—and from one situation to another (trying to negotiate a contract, planning one's life carefully).

—Howard Gardner
Harvard University

Improvement is essentially a school-by-school process, enlightened by the degree to which those associated with each school and trying to improve it have the data required for building a useful agenda.

—John I. Goodlad, Center for
Educational Renewal, University
of Washington

Standardized testing has swelled and mutated, like a creature in those old horror movies, to the point that it now threatens to swallow our schools whole. Of course, on the late, late show no one ever insists that the monster is really doing us a favor by making its victims more "accountable."

—Alfie Kohn, educational theorist

If identity and integrity are more fundamental to good teaching than technique—and if we want to grow as teachers—we must do something alien to academic culture: we must talk to each other about our inner lives—risky stuff in a profession that fears the personal and seeks safety in the technical, the distant, the abstract.

—Parker J. Palmer, Founder, Fetzer
Institute Teacher Formation Program

Too few leaders understand that America's schools have never performed as we would now have them perform, and of those who do understand these facts, too many behave defensively when confronted with the charge that today's schools are not meeting the needs of modern society.

—Phillip C. Schlechty, Founder, Center
for Leadership in School Reform

Far from creating independent thinkers, schools have always, throughout history, played an institutional role in a system of

control and coercion. And once you are well educated, you have already been socialized in ways that support the power structure, which, in turn, rewards you immensely.

—Noam Chomsky, Massachusetts
Institute of Technology

If the school has one main goal, a goal that guides the establishment and priority of all others, it should be to promote the growth of students as healthy, competent, moral people. This is a huge task to which all others are properly subordinated. We cannot ignore our children—their purposes, anxieties, and relationships— in the service of making them more competent in academic skills. My position is not anti-intellectual. It is a matter of setting priorities. Intellectual development is important, but it cannot be the first priority of schools.

—Nel Noddings, Stanford University

Teaching is the form or the act of knowing, which the professor or educator exercises; it takes as its witness the student. This act of knowing is given to the student as a testimony, so that the student will not merely act as a learner. In other words, teaching is the form that the teacher or educator possesses to bear witness to the student on what knowing is, so that the student will also know instead of simply learn.

—Paulo Freire (1921-1997), Author
Pedagogy of the Oppressed

There is no more delicious elixir than being authentically needed. Telling a kid that he or she can help solve a problem is a form of profound respect.

—Theodore R. Sizer, Founder
Coalition of Essential Schools

I am interested in having schools be ready for the differences that their school entrants will display across the entire range of competencies. If we notice children taking different paths we can interact with their different journeys just as we would alter our talking to adapt to our listeners and in a couple of years expect them to arrive at common outcomes.

—Marie M. Clay, Founder
Reading Recovery

Charismatic leaders inadvertently often do more harm than good because, at best, they provide episodic involvement followed by frustrated or despondent dependency. Superhuman leaders also do us another disservice: they are role models who can never be emulated by large numbers. Deep and sustained reform depends on many of us, not just on the very few who are destined to be extraordinary.

—Michael Fullan, Ontario Institute
for Studies in Education, University
of Toronto

The only good kind of instruction is that which marches ahead of development and leads it.

—L.S. Vygotsky (1896-1934), Author
Thought and Language

During the civil rights struggle of the 1960s, we recognized that equality in America depended upon legal equality. Now, in the Information Age, we must recognize that equality depends upon educational quality for all children. That is why it is time to declare that a quality education for every child is the new civil right.

—Richard W. Riley, former
U.S. Secretary of Education

The decontextualized multiple-choice standardized exam has become more than a measuring instrument; it has become the shield behind which people are hiding to avoid transforming our educational institutions.

—David Thornburg, Founder
The Thornburg Center

School finance issues and structures are changing. Today, school finance analysts must understand how effective education systems operate. Working with education program experts, they need to identify the cost of programs that work—that teach students to high standards—and the costs and structures of teacher salary systems that can find and keep high-quality teachers. And they must incorporate these cost findings into school finance structures

that provide each district and school with an adequate level of fiscal resources. Schools then need to use those resources for those effective programs, even if that requires significant program change and resource reallocation.

—Allan Odden, University
of Wisconsin

You need to map the political terrain of an organization before making your move. Someone's position on the organizational chart does not necessarily tell you how much they know or how much influence they have.

—Lee G. Bolman, University of
Missouri at Kansas City; and
Terrence E. Deal, University of
Southern California

Quality schoolwork (and the quality life that results from it) can only be achieved in a warm, supportive classroom environment. It cannot exist if there is an adversarial relationship between those who teach and those who are asked to learn. Not only need there be a strong, friendly feeling between teacher and students, the same feeling is necessary among the students, teachers, and administrators. Above all, there must be trust: They must all believe that the others have their welfare in mind. Without this trust, neither students nor teachers will make the effort needed to do quality work.

—William Glasser, Founder,
The William Glasser Institute

When teachers accept common goals for students and therefore complement each other's teaching, and when supervisors work with teachers in a manner consistent with the way teachers are expected to work with students, then—and only then—does the school reach its goals.

—Carl D. Glickman, Founder
The Program for School Improvement

The effective teacher establishes good control of the class in the very first week of school. Control does not involve threats or intimidation. Control means that you know (1) what you are doing, (2) your classroom procedures, and (3) your professional responsibilities. It is urgent also that your students know that you know what you are doing. You must have everything ready and under control when school begins.

—Harry and Rosemary Wong
educational consultants

There isn't one best way of doing things, something our society very much needs to learn. We're a society that wants things to be black and white, a, b, c, or d. What other country has such a preoccupation with multiple-choice tests? Life really isn't that way.

—Robert J. Sternberg, Yale University

We invest in children because the cost to the public of sickness, ignorance, neglect, dependence, and unemployment over the long

*term exceeds the cost of preventive investment in health, education,
employed youth, and stable families.*

—Marian Wright Edelman, Founder
Children's Defense Fund

*Understanding corporations, armies, research laboratories,
transportation systems, universities, government bureaus,
and fast-food restaurant chains as formal organizations
makes sense. But the organization metaphor does not fit
the nature of school purposes, the work that schools do, the
relationships needed for serving parents and students,
the context for work that teachers need to be successful,
or the nature of effective teaching and learning
environments.*

—Thomas J. Sergiovanni
Trinity University

*Reformers exceed the speed limit for putting reforms in. An
important part of reform is explaining to parents what the problem
is, talking with them about the possible solutions and how is it
working out. I think that when reformers learn to get the teachers
on their side and get the parents on their side, we're going to see
more lasting change in classrooms.*

—David B. Tyack
Stanford University

The teaching-learning approach that works best for at-risk kids is a "gifted and talented" strategy rather than a remedial approach.

—Henry M. Levin
Stanford University

One of the evils of an abstract or remote external aim in education is that its very inapplicability in practice is likely to react into a haphazard snatching at immediate conditions. A good aim surveys the present state of experience of pupils, and forming a tentative plan of treatment, keeps the plan constantly in view and yet modifies it as conditions develop. The aim, in short, is experimental, and hence constantly growing as it is tested in action.

—John Dewey (1859-1952), Author
Democracy and Education

[A]ctual and potential leadership in schools and classrooms will either atrophy or get diverted into novel forms of resisting directives aimed at standardizing behavior and holding school people accountable. Initiative, inventiveness, and imagination among those who take the moral view of teaching will be channeled into guerrilla skirmishing, covert resistance, or apathy. Educators will resist, using methods they have used for years, in order to accomplish what they believe is necessary in their classrooms and schools.

—Larry Cuban, Stanford University

The biggest problem besetting schools is the primitive quality of human relationships among children, parents, teachers, and administrators. Many schools perpetuate infantilism. School boards infantilize superintendents; superintendents, principals; principals, teachers; and teachers, children. This leads to children and adults who frequently behave like infants, complying with authority from fear or dependence, waiting until someone's back is turned to do something "naughty." To the extent that teachers and principals together can make important school decisions, they become colleagues. They become grown-ups. They become professionals.

—Roland S. Barth, Founder
Harvard Principal Center

There are innumerable well-intentioned bank-clerk teachers who do not realize that they are serving only to dehumanize.

—Paolo Freire (1921-1997), Author
Pedagogy of the Oppressed

Those of us who work in the field of education are neither bank tellers who have little discretion nor assembly line workers whose actions are largely repetitive. Each child we teach is wonderfully unique, and each requires us to use in our work that most exquisite of human capacities, the ability to make judgments in the absence of rules. Although good teaching uses routines, it is seldom routine. Good teaching depends on sensibility and imagination. It courts surprise. It profits from caring. In short, good teaching is an artistic affair.

—Elliot W. Eisner, Stanford University

He who would say that the principle of liberty informs the pedagogy of today, would make us smile as at a child who, before the box of mounted butterflies, should insist that they were alive and could fly.

—Maria Montessori (1870-1952)
Author, *The Montessori Method*

School systems' ongoing search for a teacher-proof curriculum continues to be grounded in mistrust of teachers' capabilities to make sound decisions about how and what students should be taught. Unfortunately, a teacher-proof curriculum is also student-proof.

—Linda Darling-Hammond
Stanford University

Teaching depends on human interactions over long periods of time and on the transmission of wisdom, as well as the gradual elimination of practices that are ineffective. The educational systems that we admire all over the world aren't based on scientific research; they're the ones where skilled practitioners have cultivated wise procedures over the generations and passed them on to their successors carefully and critically. Attempts to create teacher-proof systems are destined to fail. We need to honor the craft of teaching, not try to eliminate it by scientific manipulations.

—Howard Gardner
Harvard University

Serious intellectual work dramatically captures the mind and dramatically lessens boredom. A youngster who is engaged in school is a youngster who stays in school. The youngster who stays in school is the youngster the faculty knows. If the faculty is deployed in such a way that teachers can act on that knowledge, you will see a dramatic drop in violence but, more importantly, a dramatic increase in the sense of agency, self-esteem and of constructive powerful behavior.

—Theodore R. Sizer, Founder
Coalition of Essential Schools

Tests have lately become a mechanism by which public officials can impose their will on schools, and they are doing so with a vengeance. . . . Our children are tested to an extent that is unprecedented in our history and unparalleled anywhere else in the world. Rather than seeing this as odd, many of us have come to take it for granted. The result is that most of today's discourse about education has been reduced to a series of crude monosyllables: "Test scores are too low. Make them go up."

—Alfie Kohn, educational theorist

Good teaching cannot be reduced to technique; good teaching comes from the identity and integrity of the teacher.

—Parker J. Palmer, Founder
Fetzer Institute Teacher
Formation Program

There are very few things that all students need to know, and it ought to be acceptable for students to reject some material in order to pursue other topics with enthusiasm.

—Nel Noddings, Stanford University

Even though the process of identifying standards has been clumsy, it has started a conversation across the United States about what students should know in different subject areas. Perhaps that's all it has done. But that's a huge step forward. The debate about whether or not academic achievement is important is over. Ten years ago, you wouldn't have had agreement that academic achievement was the central focus of public education. Today the standards movement has made this a foregone conclusion

—Robert J. Marzano
Cardinal Stritch University

We cannot solve the problems that do exist if we're distracted by problems that don't exist. Claiming that the system is failing is not only distracting, but creates the wrong climate for improvement— you don't get people to do better by telling them how lousy they are.

—Gerald W. Bracey
educational researcher

Even though critics of America's schools are often wrong in their analysis of what is wrong with these schools, they are not wrong

when they assert that the performance of America's schools is inadequate to meet the needs of modern society.

—Phillip C. Schlechty, Founder, Center
for Leadership in School Reform

What does it mean to "eradicate illiteracy"? It gives the impression of pulling out bad weeds. It's insulting. We don't need to eradicate illiteracy, but the injustice which produces it.

—Paulo Freire (1921-1997), Author
Pedagogy of the Oppressed

The instructional program needs to be designed to better help students see the connections between their academic fare and the real-world problems they will encounter. Most teachers would like to help students recognize the need for continuous learning throughout life, but conventional school schedules provide little opportunity for interdisciplinary teaching. There is also a need to give attention throughout the curriculum to themes or topics of common concern— such as environmental education, character education, or skills in writing—which now may receive attention in only one class.

—Gordon Cawelti, Educational
Research Service

It is not the experiments the teacher may demonstrate before them, or those they carry out themselves according to a pre-established procedure, that will teach students the general rules of scientific experimentation. . . . [A]n experiment not carried out by the individual himself is by definition not an experiment but mere drill

with no educational value: the details of the successive steps are not adequately understood.

—Jean Piaget (1896-1980), Author
The Origins of Intelligence in Children

If sectarian institutions are capable of providing a nonsectarian education to students, especially students who otherwise would be stuck in schools that don't work, then they should be free to compete for those students and the public dollars that come with them.

—Rod Paige, U.S. Secretary
of Education

Excessive preoccupation with the educational or the religious idiom, to the point of making one from two, leads to mischief. Education has to do with human understandings and power, religion with what lies just beyond.

—John I. Goodlad, Center for
Educational Renewal, University
of Washington

In many school districts, arts programs have been systematically dismantled. It is indeed illogical that as corporate American is putting great pressure on the schools to provide a creative workforce, they do not connect the arts to this goal. Our often-cited competitors, Japan and Germany, clearly make this necessary connection. Japan's secondary schools require five credit hours of arts education, and Germany requires seven to nine hours a year.

The United States requires zero to two hours. So much for understanding our competition.

—Gerald N. Tirozzi, Executive
Director, National Association of
Secondary School Principals

Too often, professional development is not carefully conceived to help teachers develop and use specific skills needed to increase student achievement. Also, most professional development is not rigorously evaluated to determine what teachers learned and how effectively they applied that learning in their schools and classrooms. As educators heed the call for a research-based approach to professional development, they must redesign their programs to provide an effective system of instructional support for teachers. This new approach to professional development must be linked to concrete teaching tasks, organized around problem solving, informed by research, and sustained over time.

—Gene R. Carter, Executive Director
Association for Supervision and
Curriculum Development

A principal has to be a spiritual leader. We have to help people recapture the meaning of the work, and we have to talk about the things that touch their hearts.

—Lee G. Bolman, University of
Missouri at Kansas City; and
Terrence E. Deal, University of
Southern California

A superintendent's vision does little to promote leadership for better education unless teachers, administrators, school officials, parents, and members of the community understand it, believe that it is meaningful, and know what it implies for them.

—Susan Moore Johnson
Harvard University

[S]pend a lot of time talking with your students as they work individually or in small groups. As they talk, and as you encourage them to keep talking, they will naturally try to improve the way they express themselves. As they do, you may want at times to point out places where they can improve their grammar. As you do this, try to explain the purpose of learning grammar is to improve the clarity of what they are trying to say. Students tend not to understand this and view grammar as a chore if it is taught separate from its use.

—William Glasser, Founder
The William Glasser Institute

Any attempt to introduce a change into the school involves some existing regularity, behavioral or programmatic. These regularities are in the nature of intended outcomes. It is a characteristic of the modal process of change in the school culture that the intended outcome (the change in the regularity) is rarely stated clearly, and if it is stated clearly, by the end of the change process it has managed to get lost. It certainly was not an intended outcome of the introduction of the new math that it should be taught precisely the way the old math was taught.

—Seymour B. Sarason, Yale University

No doubt the kind of intelligence measured by I.Q. tests is important in elementary and secondary school, and perhaps even in college. But once one leaves the academic niceties of a school setting, other aspects of intelligence that the I.Q. test ignores become much more important.

—Robert J. Sternberg, Yale University

If we train by conditioning responses, we obtain conditioned responses, with minimal degrees of transfer. If we teach understandings or intellectual conceptualizations, with logical interrelationships and organizations, we should obtain skilled, imaginative, problem solvers. Most teachers understand this difference. The conditioned-response route is easier, but the route through understanding is much more exciting to the learner and not only more significant but also more fruitful.

—J.P. Guilford (1897-1988), Author
The Nature of Human Intelligence

Before I stepped into my first classroom as a teacher, I thought teaching was mainly instruction, partly performing, certainly being in the front and at the center of classroom life. Later, with much chaos and some pain, I learned that this is the least of it— teaching includes a more splendorous range of actions. Teaching is instructing, advising, counseling, organizing, assessing, guiding, goading, showing, managing, modeling, coaching, disciplining, prodding, preaching, persuading, proselytizing, listening, interacting, nursing, and inspiring.

—Gloria Ladson-Billings
University of Wisconsin

Societies cannot be all generals, no soldiers. But, by our schooling patterns, we assure that soldiers' children are more likely to be soldiers and that the offspring of generals will have at least the option to be generals. If this is not so, if it is just a matter of the difficulty of assuring perfect fairness, why does the unfairness never benefit the children of the poor?

—Jonathan Kozol
educational researcher

When conservatives today speak of "choice," they have in mind choice of schools by individual parents. But choice may take a variety of forms. Communities make collective choices about education by electing school boards that set educational policy, and by voting school budgets and bonds up or down. Religious congregations may choose to create sectarian schools for their children. Students make individual choices about their education by choosing among the electives offered at their high school. One form of choice may come at the expense of another; under a parental voucher system, the non-parents in the community would be effectively stripped of their capacity to make democratic choices about the schools they pay for. As conservatives have framed the debate, the question has been, "Are you for or against choice?" But the question ought to be, "What kind of choice are you for?"

—David B. Tyack, Stanford University

What is right for your youngster may not be right for my youngster. Different kinds of schools with different emphases give people a variety of places to send their children. Not all children are always served best by a single entity. If you have money, you can say, "My child will do better in a school with more structure." Or,

"My youngster needs to be on his own feet rather than be in a school telling him where to stand." This is a good thing—choice among congeries of schools which share educational convictions.

—Theodore R. Sizer, Founder
Coalition of Essential Schools

Choice approaches provide incentives to schools to pursue market niches that are sensitive to the "private" preferences of families rather than to emphasize the common educational experience that serves as the basis for most public benefits. Thus, increasing privatization can also mean a greater focus on the private benefits of schooling than on the social or public benefits.

—Henry M. Levin
Stanford University

Unless pro-public school forces can find effective means to educate the public about the condition of education, the anti-public school lobby is almost certain to be increasingly successful in persuading policy makers to abandon public education and to embrace some form of privatization as a solution to what ails our schools.

—Phillip C. Schlechty, Founder, Center
for Leadership in School Reform

Opponents and proponents of charter schools and vouchers agree on one thing: Our schools are not accomplishing their educational mission. However they differ in their explanations for this state of

affairs, they agree that educational reform, like reforming and strengthening Medicare and the Social Security system, should be at the top of the national agenda. That point cannot be overemphasized because it reflects a degree of disappointment, among people generally, far greater than ever before in our national history.

—Seymour B. Sarason, Yale University

Teacher behaviors that otherwise seem irrational, uncaring or unproductive can emerge in a very different light once it is understood they are guilt-ridden and guilt-driven. Strategies that teachers adopt to cope with undesirable amounts of guilt can themselves lead to further undesirable consequences in teacher behavior. Guilt, in this sense, is not so much a problem in itself as a generator of further problems beyond it. In the words of Hamlet's mother: "So full of artless jealousy is guilt. It spills itself in fearing to be spilt."

—Andy Hargreaves, Boston College

The vice of externally imposed ends has deep roots. Teachers receive them from superior authorities; these authorities accept them from what is current in the community. The teachers impose them upon children. As a first consequence, the intelligence of the teacher is not free; it is confined to receiving the aims laid down from above. Too rarely is the individual teacher so free from the dictation of authoritative supervisor, textbook on methods, prescribed course of study, etc., that he can let his mind come to close quarters with the pupil's mind and the subject matter.

—John Dewey (1859-1952), Author
Democracy and Education

The foundation for school reform is often constructed out of the narrowly perceived inadequacies of those who work in schools.

—Larry Cuban, Stanford University

A tennis shoe in a laundry dryer. Probably no image captures so fully for me the life of an adult working in an elementary, middle, or senior high school. For educators, schoolwork much of the time is turbulent, heated, confused, disoriented, congested, and full of recurring bumps.

—Roland S. Barth, Founder
Harvard Principal Center

Teachers' insistence on attending to students' experiences, interests, and prior knowledge were once thought to result from tenderheartedness and a disregard for scientific methods. Now, however, these considerations are supported by cognitive research demonstrating that learning is a process of making meaning out of new or unfamiliar events in light of familiar ideas or experiences.

—Linda Darling-Hammond
Stanford University

The idea that the school is the center of teacher education is built on the realization that whatever teachers become professionally, the process is not finished when they complete their teacher education

program at age 21. Learning to teach well is a lifetime endeavor. The growth of understanding and skill in teaching terminates only when we do.

—Elliot W. Eisner, Stanford University

If you asked me should people be studying physics, or chemistry or biology or geology in high school, I would say it doesn't make the slightest bit of difference. They should study some topics, of course, but the choice is wide open—I'm interested in depth, not breadth. I'm not talking about college education; I'm just taking on K to 12. What I want when kids get through a K to 12 education is for them to have a sense of what their society thinks is true, beautiful and good; false, ugly and evil; how to think about it and how to act on the basis of your thoughts.

—Howard Gardner
Harvard University

There is no particular substantive reform I would recommend— because no single reform will account for much difference. It has to be an array of reforms orchestrated at the community level and involving a joining of schools and universities, as well as a much closer relationship between community and school than we've been having in the last few decades.

—John I. Goodlad, Center for
Educational Renewal, University
of Washington

Children who are excited about what they are doing tend to acquire the skills they need to do it well, even if the process takes a while. When interest is lacking, however, learning tends to be less permanent, less deeply rooted, less successful. Performance, we might say, is a by-product of motivation.

—Alfie Kohn, educational theorist

I don't think teachers understand the power they have to introduce young people or adult students to realities in the world that can be enlarging or ennobling. There are ways of introducing people to subjects such as poverty that will empower them to come to terms with that great issue in our society and to feel like larger human beings in the course of doing so.

—Parker J. Palmer, Founder, Fetzer
Institute Teacher Formation Program

An adequate political education should help students to make well-informed choices. I am not suggesting that students be allowed to exercise blind desire. Indeed, it is because a free society makes it possible for people to follow their blind desires (within their means) that education in a democracy must prepare students to make sound choices. To choose wisely among even fine possibilities requires information. In addition, it requires a relationship between teachers and students that will make it possible for teachers to guide each student responsibly.

—Nel Noddings, Stanford University

Higher standards without commensurate compensation will merely drive the best from the teaching ranks, rather than attract high-quality people. The commitment and interest of business need to permeate education through bad times as well as good.

—Paul D. Houston, Executive Director
American Association of School
Administrators

So what to do for low-achieving students? From an analysis of the research data, the answer seems to be this: Provide these children extra assistance, summer school if need be (something that is a lot less expensive than having the child repeat the same grade the next year), and then promote them.

—Gerald W. Bracey
educational researcher

The role of the educator is one of a tranquil possession of certitude in regard to the teaching not only of contents but also of "correct thinking." . . . One of the necessary requirements for correct thinking is a capacity for not being overly convinced of one's own certitudes.

—Paolo Freire (1921-1997), Author
Pedagogy of the Oppressed

Individual schools can become highly collaborative despite the school system they are in, but they cannot stay highly collaborative

despite their systems. Key people leave, people get transferred, and so on. Two-way, top-down/bottom-up solutions are needed in which schools and districts influence each other through a continually negotiated process and agenda.

—Michael Fullan, Ontario Institute
for Studies in Education, University
of Toronto

Success in learning a foreign language is contingent on a certain degree of maturity in the native language. The child can transfer to the new language the system of meanings he already possesses in his own. The reverse is also true—a foreign language facilitates mastering the higher forms of the native language. The child learns to see his language as one particular system among many, to view its phenomena under more general categories, and this leads to awareness of his linguistic operations. Goethe said with truth that "he who knows no foreign language does not truly know his own."

—L.S. Vygotsky (1896-1934), Author
Thought and Language

If we can detect the process of learning to read "going wrong" within a year of school entry, then it would be folly to wait several years before providing children with extra help.

—Marie M. Clay, Founder
Reading Recovery

While education is a state responsibility and a local function, it also should be a national priority.

—Richard W. Riley, former U.S.
Secretary of Education

There is no question that computers connected to the Internet can be powerful tools for communication and collaboration with colleagues. In fact, this was the motivation for creating the Internet in the first place. The deeper issue is the realization that no educator is alone. No matter what challenge faces you, there are likely many others who have encountered the same situation. By using the global network to reach out across space and time, we can each develop strategies and techniques to help our students achieve their potential.

—David Thornburg, Founder
The Thornburg Center

It will take decades for most teachers to successfully integrate computers into their daily classroom instruction. The reason goes to the heart of the problem of nonteachers asking teachers to make deep changes in their behavior without seriously considering what happens in classrooms.

—Larry Cuban
Stanford University

*Putting talented people into a confusing structure wastes their
energy and undermines their effectiveness. Structural
arrangements, like human needs, require continual attention.*

> —Lee G. Bolman, University of
> Missouri at Kansas City; and
> Terrence E. Deal, University of
> Southern California

*The single salary schedule is so resilient that one could argue
that the "steps and lanes" of the salary schedule are the DNA of
teacher pay.*

> —Allan Odden, University
> of Wisconsin

*The best way to teach a skill-based curriculum is to relate what you
are trying to teach to the real world. For example, all of us,
including students, are interested in some of the news of the day. It
is called news because we can relate it to our lives. AIDS, or HIV,
is almost always in the news. Starting with this interesting
information, you could take your students into almost every nook
and cranny of medical biology by teaching them about AIDS.*

> —William Glasser, Founder
> The William Glasser Institute

*What is democratic learning? Democratic learning aims for
freedom of expression, pursuit of truth in the marketplace of ideas,*

individual and group choices, student activity and participation, associative learning, and the application, demonstration, and contribution of learning to immediate and larger communities. Such efforts are made in the context of justice and equality for all, a consideration of individual liberty and group freedom, and respect for the authority and responsibility of teachers in setting conditions for developmental learning.

—Carl D. Glickman, Founder, The
Program for School Improvement

Snap judgments are often poor judgments. Jumping into problems without adequate reflection is likely to lead to false starts and erroneous conclusions. Yet timed tests often force a person to solve problems impulsively. But most of us encounter few significant problems in work or personal life that demand an answer in only 5 or even 50 seconds, the typical time allotted for a solution on a standardized test

—Robert J. Sternberg, Yale University

Our heart goes out to all the neophyte teachers who want to be their students' friend. Be friendly, caring, loving, and sensitive, but do not be their friend. They have enough on their hands with their own friends. The students of today need you to be an adult role model that they can look to with admiration and pride.

—Harry and Rosemary Wong,
educational consultants

Thorough homework—good fact-finding coupled with good analysis—is essential if good remedies are to follow and if an effective case is to be made for a particular cause. Too many good intentions and causes are wrecked, and victims left unhelped, by fiery rhetoric, political grandstanding, and simplistic remedies that sometimes create more problems than they solve. Being soft-hearted, as many label those who advocate for greater attention to human needs, does not mean being soft-headed.

—Marian Wright Edelman, Founder
Children's Defense Fund

For schools to work well, we need theories of leadership that recognize the capacity of parents, teachers, administrators, and students to sacrifice their own needs for causes they believe in. We need theories of leadership that acknowledge that parents, teachers, administrators, and students are more norm-referenced decision makers than individual decision makers. Instead of making individual calculations based on self-interest, we should acknowledge that people are responsive to norms, values, and beliefs that define the standard for living together as a group and that provide them with meaning and significance.

—Thomas J. Sergiovanni
Trinity University

A free-for-all competition for a scarce resource—fine schools— between families that start out highly unequal in information, influence, and resources hardly seems likely to benefit the have-nots, though it might be attractive to the haves.

—David B. Tyack, Stanford University

There is no one who can say that this or that is the best way to know things, to feel things, to see things, to remember things, to apply things, to connect things and that no other will do as well. In fact, to make such a claim is to trivialize learning, to reduce it to a mechanical skill.

—Neil Postman (1931–2003), Author
Teaching as a Subversive Activity

The chief source of the "problem of discipline" in schools is that the teacher has often to spend the larger part of the time in suppressing the bodily activities which take the mind away from its material. . . . It may be seriously asserted that a chief cause for the remarkable achievements of Greek education was that it was never misled by false notions into an attempted separation of mind and body.

—John Dewey (1859-1952), Author
Democracy and Education

To some extent we are faced with a choice: hire pedestrian, mediocre teachers who comply willingly with imposed uniformities, or hire highly qualified, imaginative teachers who demand a great deal of instructional autonomy. I'm not sure we can have it both ways: there just aren't many highly qualified sheep to teach in our schools.

—Roland S. Barth, Founder, Harvard
Principal Center

Personalization is not just "nice" for students; it is essential for serious teaching and learning.

—Linda Darling-Hammond
Stanford University

Read 10 good articles describing 10 "effective" schools and you will have read little about effective programs and a great deal about effective people. These schools "work" because the people driving them are able. Nothing else, ultimately, is very important.

—Theodore R. Sizer, Founder
Coalition of Essential Schools

The kind of schools we need would be staffed by teachers who are as interested in the questions students ask after a unit of study as they are in the answers students give. On the whole, schools are highly answer-oriented. Teachers have the questions, and students are to have the answers. Even with a problem-solving approach, the focus of attention is on the student's ability to solve a problem that someone else has posed. Yet the most intellectually demanding tasks lie not so much in solving problems as in posing questions.

—Elliot W. Eisner, Stanford University

People say, well, you've got to read 500 books before you get through high school—I say bull! You've got to read a small number

of good books very carefully, and learn how to think about books.
You have the rest of your life to read Moby Dick, *or* Silas Marner
or The Color Purple.

—Howard Gardner
Harvard University

Many of the teachers and parents who grumble that kids "just
don't take responsibility" spend their days ordering kids around—
as though children could learn how to make good decisions by
following directions.

—Alfie Kohn, educational theorist

Bad teachers distance themselves from the subject they are
teaching—and in the process, from their students. Good teachers
join self and subject and students in the fabric of life.

—Parker J. Palmer, Founder, Fetzer
Institute Teacher Formation Program

American public schools are better at doing what they were
designed to do than ever in the past. Unfortunately, what the
schools were designed to do is no longer serving the needs of
American society. The schools were designed to ensure that all
citizens will be basically literate (able to decode words), that most
will be functionally literate (able to read well), and that a
relatively small number (20 percent or less) will be able

*to meet reasonably high academic standards. This goal has
been achieved.*

—Phillip C. Schlechty, Founder, Center
for Leadership in School Reform

*Caring implies a continuous search for competence. When we care,
we want to do our very best for the objects of our care. To have as
our educational goal the production of caring, competent, loving,
and lovable people is not anti-intellectual. Rather, it demonstrates
respect for the full range of human talents. Not all human beings
are good at or interested in mathematics, science, or British
literature. But all humans can be helped to lead lives of deep
concern for others, for the natural world and its creatures, and for
the preservation of the human-made world.*

—Nel Noddings, Stanford University

*What everyone appears to want for students—a wide array of
learning opportunities that engage students in experiencing,
creating, and solving real problems, using their own experiences,
and working with others—is for some reason denied to teachers
when they are the learners. In the traditional view of staff
development, workshops and conferences conducted outside the
school count, but authentic opportunities to learn from and with
colleagues inside the school do not.*

—Ann Lieberman
Columbia University

The market theory underlying the use of choice has limited application to schools. Theoretically, a true market is infinitely expandable. It is possible, in theory, to sell, say, Coca-Cola to everyone. Schools by their very nature, however, have limited potential for expansion. Some have argued that schools will "spring up" like fast food stores and gas stations where there is a market for them. But it is telling that the people who make such arguments find their analogies in institutions that use unskilled labor and pay low wages.

—Gerald W. Bracey
educational researcher

It is not the child as a physical but as a psychic being that can provide a strong impetus to the betterment of mankind. It is the spirit of the child that can determine the course of human progress and lead it perhaps even to a higher form of civilization.

—Maria Montessori (1870-1952)
Author, *The Montessori Method*

We have to make classes more lively, interesting, challenging for students. Helping teachers find ways to get kids interested in the subject is the big topic.

—Gordon Cawelti, Educational
Research Service

Should passage from one stage of development be accelerated or not? To be sure, all education, in one way or another, is just such

an acceleration, but it remains to be decided to what extent it is beneficial. It is not without significance that it takes man much longer to reach maturity than the other animals. Consequently, it is highly probable that there is an optimum rate of development, to exceed or fall behind which would be equally harmful. But we do not know its laws, and on this point as well it will be up to future research to enlighten us.

—Jean Piaget (1896-1980)
Author, *The Origins of Intelligence in Children*

No idea in politics has hurt children more than the false and misleading idea that the quality of education is determined by how much we spend. For three decades, our nation and our political parties have debated and contentiously fought over the issue of money in education. But the facts are simple: What determines a child's future isn't how much is spent, but how wisely that money is spent.

—Rod Paige, U.S. Secretary
of Education

I actually do have a degree in divinity, and oftentimes people say that maybe the only way we can really get more money for schools is to pray.

—Allan Odden, University
of Wisconsin

Cultures are created over time as people face challenges, solve problems, and try to make sense out of their experiences. The present is always sculpted by powerful echoes from the past. Frequent glances in a school's rearview mirror are as necessary as having a vision of the future.

—Lee G. Bolman, University of
Missouri at Kansas City; and
Terrence E. Deal, University of
Southern California

In the minds of most citizens, math and history, even poorly learned, are more important than the arts. This is unfortunate, because in the real world there are huge numbers of jobs in the arts. Entertainment (all art) is our biggest export, yet we downgrade these subjects in school.

—William Glasser, Founder
The William Glasser Institute

There needs to be a realization that through a comprehensive arts education program students' lives are enriched, their mental capacities challenged, their appreciation of the environment increased and their understanding of the profound forms of human achievement intensified. Such is the power and wonder of the arts!

—Gerald N. Tirozzi, Executive
Director, National Association of
Secondary School Principals

*It is generally believed that as a result of collective bargaining
there have been big changes in the relative authority of principals
and teachers. In fact, an analysis of contract language confirms
that teachers have indeed won access to more formal powers.
. . . But it would be misleading to assume that the gains
in formal authority won by teachers at the bargaining table have
been translated directly into powers that are exercised in the
schools. Nor is it accurate to conclude that the formal constraints
on principals inevitably reduce their capacity to manage
staff.*

—Susan Moore Johnson
Harvard University

*Because one of the stated purposes of charter schools is that if
successful they will have a positive influential impact on existing
schools, it is essential that ways be developed whereby informal
relationships between personnel in charter schools and those in
"regular" schools can be ongoing, without impinging on the
freedom of charter schools to do what they said they would do.
Without such informal relationships charter schools become
places isolated from the educational system they hope to
influence.*

—Seymour B. Sarason
Yale University

*Where assessment is educative, we hear classroom and hallway
conversations that are different than those heard in schools that use
traditional assessment methods. Students are no longer asking
teachers, "Is this what you want?" or "Is this going to be on the*

test?" Instead, learning goals and standards are so clearly spelled out that students understand what they are expected to learn. Moreover, these goals and standards are spelled out in terms of performance so that students know how they are expected to demonstrate their learning.

—Grant P. Wiggins, Co-founder
Center on Learning, Assessment and
School Structure

Creative thinking and problem solving are essentially one and the same phenomenon. If this linkage takes some of the glamour out of the concept of creative thinking, it also gives a much needed emphasis to the concept of problem solving. In solving a problem, an individual is forced to do something new in the way of behavior; new for him, that is. Unless a situation requires something new of him, he has no problems. To the extent that problem solving includes something new or novel it involves creative thinking.

—J.P. Guilford (1897-1988), Author
The Nature of Human Intelligence

A life in teaching is a stitched-together affair, a crazy quilt of odd pieces and scrounged materials, equal parts invention and imposition. To make a life in teaching is largely to find your own way, to follow this or that thread, to work until your fingers ache, your mind feels as if it will unravel, and your eyes give out, and to make mistakes and then rework large pieces. It is sometimes tedious and demanding, confusing and uncertain, and yet it is often creative and dazzling: Surprising splashes of color can suddenly

appear at its center; unexpected patterns can emerge and lend the whole affair a sense of grace and purpose and possibility.

—Gloria Ladson-Billings
University of Wisconsin

The most gentle and least manipulative of people often prove to be intolerable "operators" once they are faced with something like two thousand children and four thousand angry parents. Even those people who care the most about the personal well-being of young children turn easily into political performers once they are confronted with the possibilities for political machination that are created by a venture that involves so many people and so much publicity.

—Jonathan Kozol
educational researcher

Metaphors of the market can mask abiding inequalities and obscure the civic purposes of schooling. Americans participate in a marketplace economy, but they are also members of a democratic polity. Public education allows Americans to make choices about schools that reflect not just what works for the individual or family, but for the community or even the whole society.

—David B. Tyack, Stanford University

Teacher cultures, the relationships between teacher and their colleagues, are among the most educationally significant aspects of

teachers' lives and work. They provide a vital context for teacher development and for the ways that teachers teach. What goes on inside the teacher's classroom cannot be divorced from the relations that are forged outside it.

—Andy Hargreaves, Boston College

No one has ever explained why children are so full of questions outside of the school (so that they pester grown-up persons if they get any encouragement), and the conspicuous absence of display of curiosity about the subject matter of school lessons. Reflection on this striking contrast will throw light upon the question of how far customary school conditions supply a context of experience in which problems naturally suggest themselves. . . . There must be more actual material, more stuff, more appliances, and more opportunities for doing things, before the gap can be overcome.

—John Dewey (1859-1952), Author
Democracy and Education

It is time to recognize that getting teachers to integrate technology smoothly into daily learning—which is the proper goal for using computers—is more than UPS delivering machines to the schoolhouse door; it is more than having teacher workshops or pressing universities to alter their teacher education programs. Changing what teachers do in their classrooms requires paying attention to the daily workplace conditions and constant external demands, and the inherent unreliability of the innovations themselves.

—Larry Cuban, Stanford University

Schools and school systems are unsuccessful at many things. One area in which they excel is in promoting a culture of dependency. "What am I supposed to do?" the superintendent must ask of the local and state boards. Then memos go out to principals who respond, "What am I supposed to do?" Principals, in turn, put memos in teachers' boxes—or in their e-mail. Teachers respond, "What am I supposed to do?" Teachers in turn put assignments on pupils; desks which are greeted by students with, "What am I supposed to do?" And so it goes.

—Roland S. Barth, Founder
Harvard Principal Center

Right now we have children accountable to the government to pass the tests. What is the government accountable for to the children?

—Linda Darling-Hammond
Stanford University

Where the public political arena ends and the educational arena begins is a boundary that never existed, but it took teacher strikes and collective bargaining to underline the realities. Schools are physically bounded structures. In all other respects their boundaries are porous to a degree their physical appearance and the traditional concept of a school system obscure.

—Seymour B. Sarason, Yale University

The notion that there should be some sort of a firewall between educational decisions and the vagaries of immediate politics is

*today considered quaint. The unmoderated politicization of the
curriculum appears in some quarters to be a settled fact.*

—Theodore R. Sizer, Founder
Coalition of Essential Schools

*Arguably, the alternative to a student-centered classroom today
is not one that is teacher centered but one that is legislature
centered.*

—Alfie Kohn, educational theorist

*Educators may believe it is in their self-interest to keep
policymakers out of educational business, but what is truly in their
self-interest is to support a conception of policy that would
undergird rather than undermine school-based improvement. The
alternatives may be grim: a few excellent schools amidst a failing
system or even abandonment of the public system and the
privatization of schooling.*

—Susan H. Fuhrman, University
of Pennsylvania

*It is interesting and significant that kindergarten teachers often
encourage children to use their senses to explore materials and
tasks. When the educational stakes are still modest, there is time
and even merit for such activities, but once the child moves into
the first grade, the grade in which the "real" business of schooling*

begins in earnest, teachers seem to have less time for such matters. Grade-earning and teacher-pleasing gradually become more important to children than securing the satisfactions a sensuous world makes possible.

—Elliot W. Eisner, Stanford University

Extraordinariness is most likely to emerge if aspiring individuals are exposed to extraordinary models; ponder the lessons embodied in those models; and have the opportunity to enact critical practices in a relatively protected setting.

—Howard Gardner
Harvard University

If teaching our young in schools became a lifelong professional career—adequately rewarded and supported, with decision-making authority commensurate with responsibility—teacher shortages would fade away.

—John I. Goodlad, Center for
Educational Renewal, University
of Washington

Teaching tugs at the heart, opens the heart, even breaks the heart— and the more one loves teaching, the more heartbreaking it can be. The courage to teach is the courage to keep one's heart open in those very moments when the heart is asked to hold more than it is

able so that teacher and students and subject can be woven into the fabric of community that learning, and living, require.

—Parker J. Palmer, Founder, Fetzer
Institute Teacher Formation Program

The diverse needs and interests that plague the public schools today are no more reconcilable in the private schools than in the public schools. In the short run, private schools can control diversity through exclusion. This works for a while, but eventually it leads to Balkanization and the destruction of democracy. Unfortunately, by the time it becomes clear that the problems are systems problems, rather than a public school-private school issue, the dismantling of our educational system will be so far along that, like Humpty Dumpty, the system will not be capable of being put back together again.

—Phillip C. Schlechty, Founder, Center
for Leadership in School Reform

When some of us object strongly to the coercion inherent in a standardized curriculum, defenders often suppose that we are recommending a permissive, "hands-off" freedom for students. In fact, what we are recommending is something much more demanding and realistic. We are recommending a system of teacher counseling and guidance that approximates parental interest in students. We reject the simple (and highly deceptive) notion that students can be given equal opportunity by force. The very notion is antithetical to democratic education.

—Nel Noddings, Stanford University

There are ways to structure learning so that it includes social, emotional, and civic skills. For example, by having children work in groups, we can help them learn to collaborate; by integrating the arts into all curricular areas, we can enhance both learning and creativity. Children can learn about sportsmanship and fair play in their physical education classes and on the playground at recess. And serving on committees or student councils gives them hands-on knowledge of how democracy works.

—Vincent L. Ferrandino, Executive
Director, National Association of
Elementary School Principals

People who know little of the nature of learning or the dynamics of classrooms—governors, legislators, state boards of education, CEOs—have decided that childhood doesn't exist, that children are merely miniature adults and so can be tried accordingly in our schools. The lasting outcomes of this mistake can only be dreaded. Throwing up on test day will be the least of them.

—Gerald W. Bracey
educational researcher

Teaching . . . can be likened to a conversation in which you listen to the speaker carefully before you reply.

—Marie M. Clay, Founder
Reading Recovery

Mandates are important. Policymakers have an obligation to set policies, establish standards, and monitor performance. But to accomplish certain kinds of purposes—in this case, important educational goals—you cannot mandate what matters, because what really matters for complex goals of change are skills, creative thinking, and committed action. Mandates are not sufficient; and the more you try to specify them, the more narrow the goals and means become. Teachers are not technicians.

—Michael Fullan, Ontario Institute
for Studies in Education, University
of Toronto

In the child's development . . . imitation and instruction play a major role. They bring out the specifically human qualities of the mind and lead the child to new developmental levels. In learning to speak, as in learning school subjects, imitation is indispensable. What the child can do in cooperation today he can do alone tomorrow. Therefore the only good kind of instruction is that which marches ahead of development and leads it; it must be aimed not so much at the ripe as at the ripening functions.

—L.S. Vygotsky (1896-1934), Author
Thought and Language

As an American with Southern roots, I have always been perplexed by the notion that 400 years of institutional prejudice against minorities could in a blink of an eye be suddenly set aside. What seems lacking is any sense of history, an honest recognition that it

takes time to correct the unfairness and inequities of the past in the world of education.

> —Richard W. Riley, former U.S.
> Secretary of Education

The argument in favor of machine-graded examinations is, primarily, that they are "cost-effective." In other words, we have chosen to define the measure of what young people can know and do on the basis of budgets.

> —David Thornburg, Founder
> The Thornburg Center

The missing piece in many violence prevention programs is character development through the cultivation of empathy and self-discipline—taught hand-in-hand with academic content. In concert with families, schools have an obligation to help students understand that learning is connected to character and the moral imperatives that bind us as individuals and societies.

> —Gene R. Carter, Executive Director
> Association for Supervision and
> Curriculum Development

Teaching is a hard job when students make an effort to learn. When they make no effort, it is an impossible one.

> —William Glasser, Founder
> The William Glasser Institute

There is, in fact, no teaching without learning.

—Paolo Freire (1921-1997), Author
Pedagogy of the Oppressed

We treat people in the schools like children, not adults. We don't treat them like professionals. The only way to attract bright people to education is to give them working conditions where they can use their minds.

—Carl D. Glickman, Founder, The
Program for School Improvement

Some critics will attack the charter school movement by pointing to a few schools that fail. But this is unfair and a mistake. Just as it is wrong to attack public education en toto *because some schools fall behind, we cannot attack a community movement because a few charters fail. Indeed, it is a measure of charter schools that they are closed when they don't meet student needs because it reminds us that our mission is to educate every child, not to perpetuate an ailing status quo.*

—Rod Paige, U.S. Secretary
of Education

[C]harter schools . . . should be required and given the funds to keep a detailed chronicle of their activities, problems, decisions, and changes in organization and rationale. Without such a chronicle we will never have a basis for judging why one charter school

achieved its goals to the extent that it did and why another charter school failed or fell far short of its mark. Such a chronicle is crucial if we seek, as we should, to use experience to alter, refine, and improve charter schools that may be created in the future; and, no less important, it should become part of the policy discussion about whether the charter school legislation should be scrapped or significantly changed.

—Seymour B. Sarason, Yale University

A capacity for autonomous learning and a thirst for unending education are more important than accurate recall or simplistic application of the particular knowledge taught. The implications for assessment are fundamental: we need to be assessing primarily for mature habits of mind and a thoughtful and effective use of knowledge.

—Grant P. Wiggins, Co-founder
Center on Learning, Assessment
and School Structure

In the world this alone is necessary—that if a man speak and act, he speak and act the truth and not a lie.

—W.E.B. Du Bois (1868-1963), Author
The Souls of Black Folk

I believe a theory for the schoolhouse needs to be aesthetically pleasing. Its language and images, for example, should be

beautiful, should evoke thoughts that are consistent with the school's human purposes and condition. I believe that a theory for the schoolhouse should encourage principals, teachers, parents and students to be self-managing, to accept responsibility for what they do, and to feel a sense of obligation and commitment to do the right thing.

—Thomas J. Sergiovanni
Trinity University

The vision of the full-service school puts the best of school reform together with all other services that children, youth, and their families need, most of which can be located in a school building. The educational mandate places responsibility on the school system to reorganize and innovate. The charge to community agencies is to bring into the school: health, mental health, employment services, child care, parent education, case management, recreation, cultural events, welfare, community policing, and whatever else may fit into the picture. . . . Though this sounds like a tall order, fraught with political and practical barriers, successful models in dozens of communities show that it can happen.

—Joy G. Dryfoos
educational researcher

Successfully overcoming anxieties about opening up to parents will not only help teachers in their improvement efforts but will also help them to turn around public attitudes toward their work. Garnering support for public education and the work of teachers is one of the paramount priorities of education reform in the 21st century. Achieving this goal will require a sea change in

attitudes toward education and taxation. Yet it is a shift that teachers can and must start to engineer right now.

—Andy Hargreaves
Boston College

A large part of the art of instruction lies in making the difficulty of new problems large enough to challenge thought, and small enough so that, in addition to the confusion naturally attending the novel elements, there shall be luminous familiar spots from which helpful suggestions may spring.

—John Dewey (1859-1952), Author
Democracy and Education

The image of teacher as craftsman/artist continues to inspire researchers, practitioners, and policymakers. It also continues to compete with the image of teacher as bureaucrat/technocrat. No single public image captures a consensus among teachers and nonteachers over what teaching should be. Among educators, however, the conception of teacher as professional merges the technical and moral images, sacrificing clarity for a blend, but one that has come to be the preferred metaphor, blurred and unaccepted by many researchers and other professions as it may be.

—Larry Cuban
Stanford University

The secret is to steal—to walk into another teacher's classroom and say, "Give me that."

—Harry Wong, educational consultant

It is seldom clear just where desirable teacher variability stops and responsibility to continuity and consistency in curriculum begins. But it is clear that diversity suggests whimsy and capriciousness, while uniformity of curriculum, teaching style, and methodology is defensible in PTA meetings. This in itself is a powerful pressure toward uniformity in the schools.

—Roland S. Barth, Founder
Harvard Principal Center

Well-prepared teachers are the most inequitably distributed school resource.

—Linda Darling-Hammond
Stanford University

To persist in claiming that some students and schools are more meritorious than others on the basis of data that fail to measure what is in fact valued is as misleading and capricious as judging the quality of a play by the design of the playbill or how full the theater is on opening night.

—Theodore R. Sizer, Founder
Coalition of Essential Schools

The implicit curriculum of a school can teach a host of intellectual and social virtues: punctuality, a willingness to work hard on tasks that are not immediately enjoyable, and the ability to defer immediate gratification in order to work for distant goals can legitimately be viewed as positive attributes of schooling. They form no formal part of the curriculum, yet they are taught in school.

—Elliot W. Eisner, Stanford University

Education is laden with human values. While almost no one disputes the medical goals of longer and healthier lives, citizens in a democracy differ deeply about the kind of education we value. How could we ever design an educational system that would please Jesse Helms, Jesse Jackson and Jesse Ventura?

—Howard Gardner
Harvard University

One feature that stands out from the stories of somewhat successful reform is the extent and continuity of funding by philanthropies (some of them corporate) in order to serve the public good. Foundation officers tend to keep a low profile, some functioning in almost complete anonymity. By contrast, the rhetoric of politically driven education reform is laced with appeals to private purpose, commonly emphasizes efficiency, and is frequently connected to the name of a governor, a CEO, or a presidential aspirant. Often these politically driven proposals not only are short-term projects, but also run counter to last year's proposals or to those of a previous administration.

—John I. Goodlad
Center for Educational Renewal
University of Washington

Every hour spent trying to improve kids' test results is an hour not spent helping students become critical, creative, curious learners.

—Alfie Kohn, educational theorist

The place to go for the best feedback is the classroom. If we could make classroom assessment and classroom reporting a better feedback mechanism, we wouldn't have to rely on external tests. We'd have valid assessment information built into our system.

—Robert J. Marzano, Cardinal
Stritch University

Our economy can no longer afford to allow children not to be able to think and reason.

—Phillip C. Schlechty, Founder, Center
for Leadership in School Reform

Any set of standards rich enough for a particular student will contain items unnecessary for many, and any set designed realistically for all will, paradoxically, be inadequate for anyone considered individually.

—Nel Noddings
Stanford University

The push for more education for all citizens is not only job-related. Society as a whole has recognized that education brings benefits other than increased skills and the salaries they command. Educated people live longer, healthier lives and may even be happier, though the nature of happiness remains elusive. In any case, one way to keep life from being nasty, brutal, and short is through schooling.

—Gerald W. Bracey
educational researcher

Through dialogue, the teacher-of-the-students and the students-of-the-teacher cease to exist and a new term emerges: teacher-student with students-teachers. The teacher is no longer merely the-one-who-teaches, but one who is himself taught in dialogue with the students, who in turn while being taught also teach. They become jointly responsible for a process in which all grow.

—Paolo Freire (1921-1997), Author
Pedagogy of the Oppressed

It is the child alone that can reveal the plan that is natural to man. But because of its delicate condition, like that of all incipient beings, the psychic life of a child needs to be protected and to be surrounded by an environment that could be compared with the wrappings placed by nature about the physical embryo.

—Maria Montessori (1870-1952)
Author, *The Montessori Method*

In order to succeed, efforts to improve instruction must focus on the existing knowledge base about effective teaching and learning.

—Gordon Cawelti, Educational
Research Service

Affirming the right of all human beings to education is to take on a far greater responsibility than simply to assure to each one reading, writing, and arithmetic capabilities; it is to guarantee fairly to each child the entire development of his mental faculties and the acquisition of knowledge and of ethical values corresponding to the exercise of these faculties until adaptation to actual social life.

—Jean Piaget, (1896-1980), Author
The Origins of Intelligence in Children

The principals of tomorrow's schools must be instructional leaders who possess the requisite skills, capacities, and commitment to lead the accountability parade, not follow it. Excellence in school leadership should be recognized as the most important component of school reform. Without leadership, the chances for systemic improvement in teaching and learning are nil.

—Gerald N. Tirozzi, Executive
Director, National Association of
Secondary School Principals

One of the most problematic issues raised in comprehensive school change has to do with cost. Most discussions of comprehensive

school reform seem to assume that such reforms can be implemented with little if any new funds. Underlying the idea of comprehensive school reform is the notion of using existing resources differently. But it is not clear whether schools need additional money to implement comprehensive school changes or whether existing funds, if reallocated, could cover the costs.

—Allan Odden, University
of Wisconsin

Even in schools with weak or threadbare cultures, it is usually possible to find some things worth celebrating. Those stories, values, traditions, heroes, or heroines provide a vital starting point for updating, reinvigorating, and reframing the school's identity and culture.

—Lee G. Bolman, University of
Missouri at Kansas City; and
Terrence E. Deal, University of
Southern California

When students say they hate school, a lot of what they are saying is that they hate being asked to work hard at something they don't value. . . . For most of them, it is easier to see the quality in what they are asked to do at McDonald's (achieve cleanliness, courtesy and promptness) than the quality of the reading and calculating they do at school.

—William Glasser, Founder
The William Glasser Institute

To develop a lasting capacity for innovation and improvement in district staff, superintendents must respect local expertise and confront fears of change with support and training.

—Susan Moore Johnson
Harvard University

Should voucher proponents come to the realization about how much money it will cost to make it possible for parents of little or modest means to use and benefit from vouchers, the proponents will lose their enthusiasm. The G.I. Bill was not cheap but it was successful. A realistic school voucher program will not be cheap. I seriously doubt that proponents are prepared for that eventuality.

—Seymour B. Sarason, Yale University

There is an inescapable moral dimension to learning (even abstract academic learning) and to our assessment of its success. An education is not merely a training; skill can be used for good or for ill, thoughtfully or thoughtlessly. A thoughtful assessment system does not seek correct answers only, therefore. It seeks evidence of worthy habits of mind; it seeks to expose and root out thoughtlessness—moral as well as intellectual thoughtlessness.

—Grant P. Wiggins, Co-founder
Center on Learning, Assessment
and School Structure

Although special courses on creative thinking have proved beneficial, our whole educational system can be of greater help by giving more attention to this subject. There is abundant opportunity to teach almost any subject in ways that call for productive thinking rather than rote memory. Even the multiplication tables can be taught in ways that give the pupil insight into properties of the number system.

—J.P. Guilford (1897-1988), Author
The Nature of Human Intelligence

When African American students attempt to achieve in school they do so at a psychic cost. Somehow many have come to equate exemplary performance in school with a loss of their African American identity; that is, doing well in school is seen as "acting white." Thus if they do not want to "act white," the only option, many believe, is to refuse to do well in school. Thus they purposely learn how not to learn.

—Gloria Ladson-Billings, University
of Wisconsin

In seeking to find a metaphor for the unequal contest that takes place in public school, advocates for equal education sometimes use the image of a tainted sports event. We have seen, for instance, the familiar image of the playing field that isn't level. Unlike a tainted sports event, however, a childhood cannot be played again. We are children only once; and, after those few years are gone, there is no second chance to make amends. In this respect, the consequences of unequal education have a terrible finality.

—Jonathan Kozol
educational researcher

Schools and recreation centers that are full of children's artwork and cultural displays tell me the people here are really engaged by what they do, while blank gray walls and poorly lit rooms tell me a different story. The décor does not always reflect the quality of the program, but it certainly provides a clue as to what might or might not be going on there.

—Joy G. Dryfoos, educational
researcher

A school's program and purpose is the last frontier of responsibility to fall to schools. I call it "Kentucky Fried Schooling." Every school is like a franchise with its own separate set of responsibilities. But are you being empowered on the unessentials . . . rather than the things that really matter?

—Andy Hargreaves, Boston College

Every recitation in every subject gives an opportunity for establishing cross connections between the subject matter of the lesson and the wider and more direct experiences of everyday life.

—John Dewey (1859-1952), Author
Democracy and Education

[C]orporate executives, public officials and the past three U.S. presidents have assumed that low test scores in urban schools resulted from bloated bureaucracies, poorly managed districts and students, teachers and principals who are slacking off when it

*comes to academic achievement. These reformers believe that
introducing more choice, competition and accountability . . . will
cure school ills. These passionate reformers, using such slogans as
"all children can learn," reject the idea that educators need more
money to improve schooling—as if uncredentialed teachers and a
lack of preschool education and health and social services are
irrelevant to learning.*

—Larry Cuban, Stanford University

*The popular slogan today is, All children can learn. To insist,
however, that all children should get the same dose of academic
English, social studies, science, and mathematics invites an
important question not addressed by the sloganeers: Why should
children learn what we insist they "can" learn? Is this the material
people really need to live intelligently, morally, and happily? Or
are arguments for traditional liberal education badly mistaken?
Worse, are they perhaps mere political maneuverings?*

—Nel Noddings, Stanford University

*By telling everyone that all children can learn, we set the stage for
the next great round of educational failure when it is revealed that
not everyone has learned. . . . None of this is to say that many
children could not learn much more than they presently do; they
could. But if we predicate reform on unrealistic assumptions, not
only do we set the stage for inevitable failure, we are prevented
from seeing the present conditions as they really are.*

—Gerald W. Bracey
educational researcher

Educational slogans serve to replace educational thought and enable school practitioners to avoid dealing with the persistent problems of practice.

—Elliot W. Eisner, Stanford University

Teachers who choose the path of teacher leadership become owners and investors in their schools, rather than mere tenants.

—Roland S. Barth, Founder
Harvard Principal Center

Kids don't start at the same place, they don't learn in the same way, and they don't learn at the same pace.

—Linda Darling-Hammond
Stanford University

In a classroom with little or no differentiated instruction, only student similarities seem to take center stage. In a differentiated classroom, commonalties are acknowledged and built upon, and student differences become important elements in teaching and learning as well. At its most basic level, differentiating instruction means "shaking up" the classroom so that students have multiple options for taking in information, making sense of ideas, and expressing what they learn.

—Carol Ann Tomlinson
University of Virginia

You work with youngsters as long as it takes, and when you try very hard within the compulsory system to bring those youngsters, all youngsters, up to clear levels of literacy and numeracy and civic understanding, for some youngsters it's going to take longer. But you stay with them. The notion that you push kids out is simply abhorrent. You don't push kids out.

—Theodore R. Sizer, Founder
Coalition of Essential Schools

We should spend less time ranking children and more time helping them to identify their natural competencies and gifts, and cultivate those. There are hundreds and hundreds of ways to succeed, and many, many different abilities that will help you get there.

—Howard Gardner
Harvard University

Perhaps the most serious bar to understanding or improving our schools is the inadequate measures we use in seeking to determine their health. We use test scores, such as those on the SAT, as though they tell us something about the condition of schools. They tell us even less about schools than a thermometer designed to measure body temperature tells us about body health.

—John I. Goodlad, Center for
Educational Renewal, University
of Washington

No one has ever demonstrated that students today get A's for the same work that used to receive B's or C's. We simply do not have the data to support such a claim. . . . The real threat to excellence isn't grade inflation at all; it's grades.

—Alfie Kohn, educational theorist

The reason schools have not improved is that they have changed so much and so often with so little effect that leaders seem baffled about what to do next.

—Phillip C. Schlechty, Founder, Center
for Leadership in School Reform

Schools have made incremental progress in an exponential world. The failure of schools today is not against a mythical golden age of the past—it is this failure to raise all our students to a higher standard for the future. Schools should be places of joy and excitement that enliven the mind, quicken curiosity and empower students to reach their highest potential. They should be places of respect and fairness where everyone has an equal chance. They should prepare students to meet an unknown future with confidence and enthusiasm.

—Paul D. Houston, Executive
Director, American Association
of School Administrators

If everyone learned, society would collapse, literally. I do not know if education so refines the senses or simply makes people allergic to

sweat, but educated people will not collect garbage, unclog sewers, scour urinals, make up beds, bus tables, etc.

—Gerald W. Bracey
educational researcher

To teach is not to transfer knowledge but to create the possibilities for the production or construction of knowledge.

—Paolo Freire (1921-1997), Author
Pedagogy of the Oppressed

Everything we do as teachers has moral overtones.

—Nel Noddings
Stanford University

To prevent reading failure teachers must have time to observe what children are able to do. This means time out from teaching, time set aside for observing. The younger the child and the poorer the reader, the more time the teacher requires for observing and for thinking about what she observes.

—Marie M. Clay, Founder
Reading Recovery

Empowering others in the school has to form a major component of the effective principal's agenda. It is becoming clearer in the research literature that complex changes in education sometimes require active (top-down or external) initiation, but if they are to go anywhere, there must be a good deal of shared control and decision making during implementation.

—Michael Fullan, Ontario Institute
for Studies in Education, University
of Toronto

Once a new teacher enters the classroom we allow a perverse "sink or swim" approach to define the first years in teaching. New teachers are usually assigned the most difficult classes in addition to all the extra-curricular activities that no one else wants to supervise. Then we wonder why we lose 22 percent of new teachers in the first three years—and close to 50 percent in our urban areas.

—Richard W. Riley, former U.S.
Secretary of Education

As educators interested in using tools effectively with children, we often get frozen with the image in the rearview mirror as the future outstrips our capacity to fathom it. Meanwhile, our children ride the crest of this wave at light speed, surfing the edges of chaos and taking advantage of every technological tool they can grasp. By the time we pause to say "Wow!" they are already looking for the next wave. While some educators are still figuring out how to include attachments with e-mail, our children have jumped on the bandwagon to peer-to-peer and engage in multiple simultaneous

message sessions while transferring files and watching MTV in the background.

—David Thornburg, Founder
The Thornburg Center

The over-identification of students of color with special needs is a knee-jerk response to a more complex problem. You can't focus on the academic side of learning until you socialize kids into the learning environment. The solution rests, at least in part, with better professional development to help educators address cultural differences in teaching delivery and classroom management.

—Gene R. Carter, Executive Director
Association for Supervision and
Curriculum Development

Good leaders, like good teachers, are as good at listening and sensing as they are at persuading and teaching. What distinguishes leadership from other types of relationships is that, when it works well, it enables people to collaborate in the service of shared visions, values, and missions. At their best, teachers, like other leaders, shape relationships that make a measurable difference in others' lives, even though those differences may be hard to assess and may not come to fruition for years after the fact.

—Lee G. Bolman, University of
Missouri at Kansas City; and
Terrence E. Deal, University of
Southern California

When American society works well, Americans extol the American spirit, the can-do economy, the courageous people, and the heroic leaders. When American society does not do well, they lambaste the schools.

—Carl D. Glickman, Founder, The
Program for School Improvement

Principals who are intent on improving staff performance are not powerless. If such principals have district office support, they may initiate actions to terminate teachers. If that support is not forthcoming, they can follow procedures to transfer poor teachers and upgrade the quality of staff within their own schools. If even transfers are unlikely, they can observe regularly and insist on high performance, thus prodding unsatisfactory teachers and encouraging others.

—Susan Moore Johnson
Harvard University

Our educational system has all of the features of a nonlearning system: It learns nothing from its failures and is incapable of learning from and then spreading its "successes." This is not explainable on the basis of an individual psychology—there are no villains who have willed this state of affairs. It is a system of parts that is not coordinated in a structural sense and among which there is little agreement about the purposes of schooling; indeed, the parts are frequently in an adversarial relationship.

—Seymour B. Sarason, Yale University

School and college offer us the socially sanctioned opportunity, indeed the obligation, to disturb and challenge students intellectually, using knowledge as a means, not an end, to engender more effective and self-reflective thought and action. That view is at odds with the habit of using uniform tests of the content of the syllabus.

—Grant P. Wiggins, Co-founder
Center on Learning, Assessment
and School Structure

All successful classrooms must have structure. I'm not saying it has to be like a prison, but once you have structure everyone knows what to do. Then, the fun begins.

—Harry Wong, educational consultant

The wiser world has learned that in youth, even as in age, the Cost of Freedom is less than the Price of Repression.

—W.E.B. Du Bois (1868-1963), Author
The Souls of Black Folk

Our society's acceptance of two unequal educational systems is putting us at risk of creating a permanent underclass.

—Joy G. Dryfoos
educational researcher

Teachers are in an unenviable position. Like social workers, their job is never really done. There are no clear criteria to indicate when work is over. In teaching, products are never finished, patients never cured, cases never closed. So in chasing their unattainable aspirations, teachers always feel they could do with more time.

—Andy Hargreaves, Boston College

The true starting point of history is always some present situation and its problems.

—John Dewey (1859-1952), Author
Democracy and Education

This concentration on test scores drains away innovation and entrepreneurial spirit from teachers and parents. Few schools will attempt any educational risk that could endanger their ranking on a state list.

—Larry Cuban, Stanford University

Everyone who works in a school is not only entitled to a unique and personal vision of the way he or she would like the school to become, but has an obligation to uncover, discover, and rediscover what that vision is and contribute it to the betterment of the school community.

—Roland S. Barth, Founder
Harvard Principal Center

Developing the ability to see beyond one's own perspective, to put oneself in the shoes of the learner and to understand the meaning of that experience in terms of learning, is perhaps the most important role of universities in the preparation of teachers. One of the great flaws of the "bright person myth" of teaching is that it presumes that anyone can teach what he or she knows to anyone else. However, people who have never studied teaching or learning often have a very difficult time understanding how to convey material that they themselves learned effortlessly and almost subconsciously.

—Linda Darling-Hammond
Stanford University

The restructuring and the invention are happening out in the schools at an incredible pace, but higher education is in the reactive mode and slow to move.

—Ann Lieberman
Columbia University

The acquisition of literacy in one form cannot be used to predict literacy in another. One might be able to "read" the meanings of slang, but not those of poetry. One might be able to experience the flight that literature makes possible and be stymied by poetry. One might find the language of biology lucid and experience literature as a morass of ambiguity that obscures rather than reveals. To talk about literacy as if it were a single skill applicable to all forms of text is to underestimate the special demands that different forms of language exact.

—Elliot W. Eisner, Stanford University

*All the basic school subjects act as formal discipline, each
facilitating the learning of the others; the psychological functions
stimulated by them develop in one complex process.*

—L.S. Vygotsky (1896-1934), Author
Thought and Language

*We must figure out how intelligence and morality can work
together to create a world in which a great variety of people will
want to live. After all, a society led by "smart" people still might
blow up itself or the rest of the world. Intelligence is valuable but,
as Ralph Waldo Emerson famously remarked, "Character is more
important than intellect." That insight applies at both the
individual and the societal levels.*

—Howard Gardner
Harvard University

*Character education requires a strong community but not
necessarily a good one.*

—Nel Noddings
Stanford University

*To relax our concern over the quality of schools when test scores
are rising is to sidestep the responsibility of examining conditions
in our schools for purposes of determining strengths and
weaknesses and taking constructive action.*

—John I. Goodlad
Center for Educational Renewal
University of Washington

Making sure that students are continually re-sorted, with excellence turned into an artificially scarce commodity, is almost perverse.

—Alfie Kohn, educational theorist

One of the reasons for the success of service learning is that when students go out and do service their own capacity to care is what kicks in. You can't work in a political campaign or serve meals to the poor without finding something to get passionate about. When that passion starts to hook one's intellect into the cognitive work itself, learning is accelerated.

—Parker J. Palmer, Founder, Fetzer
Institute Teacher Formation Program

The problem for modern times is that the nature of our economy has changed to the point at which the quality of education and the quality of mind developed in schools do make a difference in our productivity, and will grow even more important in the years ahead. Education that simply confirms status is not sufficient.

—Phillip C. Schlechty, Founder, Center
for Leadership in School Reform

I teach because I search.

—Paolo Freire (1921-1997), Author
Pedagogy of the Oppressed

People realize that if kids are given more responsibility and they can see the value in their education, they will do better. So teachers are trying to show the application of what they teach to students. For example, in class, you might study the environment in your community, your drinking water, social issues which affect your town such as poverty and minority issues. What happens is students can get involved and come up with real solutions for their community. More schools need to do this.

—Gordon Cawelti, Educational
Research Service

The school examination becomes an end in itself because it dominates the teacher's concerns, instead of fostering his natural role as one who stimulates consciences and minds, and he directs all the work of the students toward the artificial result which is success on final tests, instead of calling attention to the student's real activities and personality.

—Jean Piaget (1896-1980), Author
The Origins of Intelligence in Children

If an educational act is to be efficacious, it will be only that one which tends to help toward the complete unfolding of life.

—Maria Montessori (1870-1952)
Author, *The Montessori Method*

Before I got to Washington, I thought that Democrats adhered to entirely different ideals about education than Republicans did. To

my surprise, I discovered that Democrats and Republicans have the same goal at heart when it comes to education: giving all children access to excellent schools. They may disagree on what is the best way to reach this goal, but they are always thinking about what is best for students.

—Rod Paige, U.S. Secretary
of Education

Recent adjudications throughout the United States have reinforced the state's responsibilities of insuring integrated education. States should not, cannot, shy away from their moral obligation.

—Gerald N. Tirozzi, Executive
Director, National Association
of Secondary School Principals

With all this school reform, schools have become sterile, toxic places. They've lost their sense of purpose. There's something really special about school, and it's something that needs to be encouraged more than it is.

—Terrence E. Deal, University
of Southern California

The great problem of American public education is not that public schools are as horrible as they are often portrayed to be in the media; very few actually are. The problem of public education is its ordinariness. The issue is not how to lift public schools out of

disaster. Instead, the issue is how to allow great schools to carry on, enable ordinary schools to strive for greatness, and provide initiatives and support for inept schools to move toward competence.

—Carl D. Glickman, Founder
The Program for School Improvement

The school site is a place where teachers' values rather than union values prevail. Teachers' allegiance to their schools and to their principals often takes precedence over their allegiance to the union. Teachers resist having their schools subsumed as indistinguishable components of the larger district. They fiercely defend their autonomy and use the union and the contract as they see fit, invoking them in some cases, ignoring them in others.

—Susan Moore Johnson
Harvard University

I am not proposing to do away with the single salary schedule, which conceptually means that all teachers are paid the same if they have similar characteristics. I am simply suggesting that we may be able to move substantially beyond simply using years of experience and education credits and to a much more sophisticated approach, largely focused on providing pay increases only for higher levels of relevant knowledge, skill, and professional expertise.

—Allan Odden, University
of Wisconsin

We can afford to pay teachers better and give them more access to training and ongoing professional development even within our current budget. It means spending most of our money as European and Asian countries do and most private schools do on teaching and teachers and much less of it on administrative superstructures and football fields.

—Linda Darling-Hammond
Stanford University

The artistry of teaching finds its source in the ability to start with where the learner is, in using that starting point to build bridges to new knowledge and outlooks heretofore not in the student's ken.

—Seymour B. Sarason, Yale University

To teach students that we are serious about intellectual standards, we must always assess their ability to see the limits of what is learned; they need to have the chance to punch holes in our own or the textbook's presentation. They have a right to demand justification of our point of view. That is what a liberal education is about. It also sends the right moral message: we are both, student and teacher, subservient to rational principles of evidence and argument.

—Grant P. Wiggins, Co-founder
Center on Learning, Assessment
and School Structure

I am convinced that we do teach some students to think, but I sometimes marvel that we do as well as we do. In the first place, we have only vague ideas as to the nature of thinking. We have little actual knowledge of what specific steps should be taken in order to teach students to think. Our methods are shotgun methods, just as our intelligence tests have been shotgun tests. It is time we discarded shotguns in favor of rifles.

—J.P. Guilford (1897-1988), Author
The Nature of Human Intelligence

In a better world I would want to see schools integrated across racial, cultural, linguistic, and all other lines. But I am too much of a pragmatist to ignore the sentiment and motivation underlying the African American immersion school movement. African Americans already have separate schools. The African American immersion school movement is about taking control of those separate schools.

—Gloria Ladson-Billings
University of Wisconsin

I was once in the Arizona desert during an electrical storm, which is a fairly spectacular event. Every time there was a crash of thunder, I'd pull the bedcovers up. About halfway through the storm, I realized that thunder makes noise, but it's lightning that does the killing. I was jumping at the wrong stimulus. Let me suggest to you that a great deal of the criticism and the solutions offered about education today are based upon "thunder analysis." In many cases, we are solving the wrong problems.

—Paul D. Houston
Executive Director
American Association
of School Administrators

We cannot establish a hierarchy of values among studies. It is futile to attempt to arrange them in an order, beginning with one having least worth and going on to that of maximum value. In so far as any study has a unique or irreplaceable function in experience, in so far as it marks a characteristic enrichment of life, its worth is intrinsic or incomparable.

—John Dewey (1859-1952), Author
Democracy and Education

Petty irritations and smoldering slights seal the differences among teachers and administrators. Teacher strikes, "sick outs," and "working to the rule" register what many see as the incompatible interests of the two occupations. Uncertainty over just whose interests principals and district office staff serve arises in those places where unions of administrators form to protect their concerns. Yet teachers, principals, and superintendents entered education to, among many reasons, help children learn; they share a common purpose. They are educators.

—Larry Cuban, Stanford University

I can think of nothing so conspicuously missing in the effort to improve our schools as the continuous engagement of teachers and principals in constructing visions—in contemplating, for instance, what constitutes desirable leadership, what children should learn, and what the teaching profession might become.

—Roland S. Barth, Founder
Harvard Principal Center

Let us remember that humans develop in often unpredictable and extraordinary ways and that depending too much on any sort of "science" to judge a human's worth is exceedingly dangerous.

—Theodore R. Sizer, Founder
Coalition of Essential Schools

Intelligence is too important to be left to the intelligence testers.

—Howard Gardner
Harvard University

The school best prepared for tomorrow is the school best geared for today. It is a school for all seasons, engaging all of its students in as many domains of human experience as it can encompass. It is a school so committed to its comprehensive mission of preparing the young to participate broadly in the human conversation that democratic societies seek to sustain that it is not diverted into the narrowing of focus that devotion to some utilitarian narrative of schooling requires.

—John I. Goodlad, Center for
Educational Renewal, University
of Washington

To evaluate schools properly, visit them. Look for kids exchanging ideas, designing projects, thinking deeply—not hunched over worksheets or listening passively to lectures. Observation isn't just

cheaper than hiring fancy firms to report test scores. It's more meaningful.

—Alfie Kohn, educational theorist

Education is no longer what one receives as a result of participating in American life. High-quality education is what one must have if one is to participate in any meaningful way. Therefore, education has ceased being merely a part of the American dream: education is the key to the dream.

—Phillip C. Schlechty, Founder, Center
for Leadership in School Reform

The student is infinitely more important than the subject-matter.

—Nel Noddings, Stanford University

Principals must find innovative ways to get involved with their communities and to restore the community school to its central place in American life. To do so, they must be prepared to share decision making with school-based councils, to work closely with social service agencies to provide services needed by at-risk children and their families, to form partnerships with community businesses and organizations, and to raise funds to supplement skimpy school budgets.

—Vincent L. Ferrandino, Executive
Director, National Association of
Elementary School Principals

Simply showing and explaining the school to the community is not enough; the community must be truly involved. And by this, I mean more than bake sales and booster clubs.

—Dennis Littky, Founder
The Big Picture Company

In addition to the schools' being the focal point for social problems, the church and family are in decline. Many consider politics a cesspool of corruption and self-interest. Every day brings some astonishing new tale of fraud and malfeasance in business. Schools are refuges of integrity and fair play.

—Gerald W. Bracey
educational researcher

In the process of the ongoing education of teachers, the essential moment is that of critical reflection on one's practice.

—Paolo Freire (1921-1997), Author
Pedagogy of the Oppressed

Because we invite children into formal education we must give up the idea that "they ripen and mature so that after a while they begin to read." This is not true. Teachers and schools are engineering certain transitions. I think this concept is very important. It gets us away from the idea of the reception class teacher as one who is just minding children until they mature, at

which point they can be moved on to a teacher who is really going to do some work with them.

—Marie M. Clay, Founder
Reading Recovery

Evidence in both business and education indicates that effective leaders have "a bias for action." They have an overall sense of direction, and start into action as soon as possible, establishing small scale examples, adapting, refining, improving quality, expanding, reshaping as the process unfolds. This strategy might be summed up as "start small: think big," or the way to get better at implementation planning is more by doing than planning.

—Michael Fullan, Ontario Institute
for Studies in Education
University of Toronto

Like all forms of loosely institutionalized power which may not be delegated to representatives, strictly academic power can only be accumulated and maintained at the cost of constant and heavy expenditure of time.

—Pierre Bourdieu (1930-2002), Author
Homo Academicus

The history of language clearly shows that complex thinking with all its peculiarities is the very foundation of linguistic development.

—L.S. Vygotsky (1896-1934), Author
Thought and Language

School districts usually find a way to put somebody in front of every classroom, and that is the problem. Too many school districts are sacrificing quality for quantity to meet the immediate demand of putting a warm body in front of a classroom. This is a mistake.

—Richard W. Riley, former U.S.
Secretary of Education

In the past you could have all the children using the encyclopedia if all the children were looking at different volumes. Now that we have encyclopedias on the Web, we can have several children looking at the exact same thing at the same time. Non-rival assets are of tremendous value to education.

—David Thornburg, Founder
The Thornburg Center

Teaching is a very lonely occupation and that loneliness often translates into a declining ability to do the job well.

—Parker J. Palmer, Founder, Fetzer
Institute Teacher Formation Program

Teachers often feel isolated and trapped in their classrooms. They are surrounded and often overwhelmed by their students, each with a complicated array of needs and talents. Yet they often feel deeply lonely. They are starved for the opportunity to talk openly with other adults who can really understand what their life is like.

Teachers can become collaborators; they can be allies and guides for each other. They can help each other through reflection and dialogue.

—Lee G. Bolman, University of
Missouri at Kansas City; and
Terrence E. Deal, University of
Southern California

I don't think people who haven't worked in schools can comprehend the intensity of the work, the emotional involvement, the non-stop demands. You really do need time to decompress.

—Susan Moore Johnson
Harvard University

You can go into any faculty lounge in the country and hear enough student bashing to last you for the rest of your life. Why? Because we don't have good ways of supporting one another when we are vulnerable. And, we all too often go to the lowest common denominator, which is blaming all those awful students for our plight.

—Parker J. Palmer, Founder, Fetzer
Institute Teacher Formation Program

Principals need to be prepared to handle the various situations they face in a day. Theory is important, but aspiring principals must be shown that most of what they will be facing will not come out of a book. They must be prepared to be open-minded and handle each

situation as it comes. Working in collaboration with school districts to create mentoring programs is important. Principals need a network of peers to alleviate the isolation and helplessness many feel.

—Thomas J. Sergiovanni
Trinity University

The difference between the teacher as a solitary figure behind a closed door and the teacher as steward of a school involves a profound shift in personality and character. The change in the way we train teachers will have to be equally profound.

—John I. Goodlad, Center for
Educational Renewal, University
of Washington

If our schools were to focus on the main goal of citizenship and democracy and show students how to connect learning with the real issues of their surroundings, then more students would learn how to write cogent compositions, would learn basic skills, would use higher-order thinking, would learn aesthetic appreciation, would excel in academics, and would graduate.

—Carl D. Glickman, Founder, The
Program for School Improvement

If you ask schoolteachers to justify the existence of an elementary, middle, or high school, the answer will be that it is for students; it

is not for the learning and development of teachers. Yet if contexts for productive learning do not exist for teachers, they cannot create and sustain that context for students.

—Seymour B. Sarason, Yale University

Standards don't mean anything until you tell me how you will measure it and how to teach to it. Unless students and teachers get better feedback, the scores aren't going to change. In school, you get told to do stuff and you're not sure where it's headed. Students deserve better. Everyone should know what's expected. No surprises, no excuses. That's what it is like in the real world.

—Grant P. Wiggins, Co-founder
Center on Learning, Assessment
and School Structure

The No. 1 problem in education is not discipline. It's a lack of routines and procedures. You have to have a plan.

—Harry Wong, educational
consultant

We must accept equality or die. What we must also do is to lay down a line of thought and action which will accomplish two things: The utter disappearance of color discrimination in American life and the preservation of African history and culture

as a valuable contribution to modern civilization as it was to medieval and ancient civilization.

—W.E.B. Du Bois (1868-1963), Author
The Souls of Black Folk

The nation, for all practice and intent, has turned its back upon the moral implications, if not yet the legal ramifications, of the Brown [v. Board of Education] *decision. The struggle being waged today, where there is any struggle being waged at all, is closer to the one that was addressed in 1896 in* Plessy v. Ferguson, *in which the court accepted segregated institutions for black people, stipulating only that they must be equal to those open to white people. The dual society, at least in public education, seems in general to be unquestioned.*

—Jonathan Kozol
educational researcher

Some educators say a "good" education is one that ensures that all students learn certain core information and master certain competencies. Others define a "good" education as one that helps students maximize their capacity as learners.

—Carol Ann Tomlinson
University of Virginia

If there is any agreement among standardized-test designers, it is that, over time, teachers and administrators become familiar with

the skills being tested, allocate time to prepare their students and, voila!, test scores rise. Test makers then re-norm their tests to make them harder, and policymakers choose different tests. Voila! Test scores dip. Teachers are blamed, and the cycle repeats itself. Ethnic and racial gaps in academic achievement persist.

—Larry Cuban, Stanford University

There is nothing at all wrong with testing, or with the state as well as parents wanting to know just how each child is learning. Good teachers "test" daily. Rather, it's the simplistic mechanization of this practice that is pernicious.

—Theodore R. Sizer, Founder
Coalition of Essential Schools

Only a school that is hospitable to adult learning can be a good place for students to learn. A community of learners implies that school is a context for everyone's lifelong growth, not just for growth among K-12 students. Adult learning is not only a means toward the end of student learning, but also an important objective in its own right.

—Roland S. Barth, Founder
Harvard Principal Center

The education challenge facing the U.S. is not that its schools are not as good as they once were. It is that schools must help the vast

majority of young people reach levels of skill and competence that were once thought to be within the reach of only a few.

—Linda Darling-Hammond
Stanford University

In education, surprise ought to be seen not as a limitation but as the mark of creative work. Surprise breeds freshness and discovery. We ought to be creating conditions in school that enable students to pursue what is distinctive about themselves; we ought to want them to retain their personal signatures, their particular ways of seeing things.

—Elliot W. Eisner, Stanford University

Poetry has historically been allied with religion and morals; it has served the purpose of penetrating the mysterious depths of things. It has an enormous patriotic value. Homer to the Greeks was a Bible, a textbook of morals, a history, and a national inspiration. In any case, it may be said that an education which does not succeed in making poetry a resource in the business of life as well as in its leisure, has something the matter with it—or else the poetry is artificial poetry.

—John Dewey (1859-1952), Author
Democracy and Education

Nowadays no one person can learn everything there is to learn. We would all like, as Renaissance men and women, to know

everything, or at least to believe in the potential of knowing everything, but that ideal clearly is not possible anymore. Choice is therefore inevitable, and one of the things that I want to argue is that the choices that we make for ourselves, and for the people who are under our charge, might as well be informed choices.

—Howard Gardner
Harvard University

Teaching is very much a process of creating an ethos in which one's students develop and enjoy as many dimensions of their lives as possible. They fashion new aspects and add to others, but if they perceive the activities in which they engage only as chores to be finished so that they can go out to play, the teacher is denied the satisfaction of creating a fruitful ethos. It often is said that the joy of teaching school is seeing children learn. But the ultimate satisfaction in teaching is derived from evidence that the sum of what one did to create a productive ethos did, indeed, do that.

—John I. Goodlad, Center for
Educational Renewal, University
of Washington

Anyone who opposes annual testing of students is an apologist for a broken system of education that dismisses certain children and classes of children as unteachable. The time has come for an end to the excuses, for the sake of the system and the children trapped inside.

—Rod Paige, U.S. Secretary
of Education

Enthusiasm for testing seems to grow as you move away from the students, going from teacher to principal to central office administrator to school board member to legislator, governor, and president. Those for whom classroom visits are occasional photo opportunities are most likely to demonstrate an unlimited zeal for testing.

—Alfie Kohn, educational theorist

The power of our mentors is not necessarily in the models of good teaching they gave us, models that may turn out to have little to do with who we are as teachers. Their power is in their capacity to awaken a truth within us, a truth we can reclaim years later by recalling their impact on our lives. If we discovered a teacher's heart in ourselves by meeting a great teacher, recalling that meeting may help us take heart in teaching once more.

—Parker J. Palmer, Founder, Fetzer
Institute Teacher Formation Program

It is past time for educational reformers in America to acknowledge that they are confronted with a choice. They either must invent a system of education that can achieve the ends Americans set for their schools—that is, high-quality academic education for all children regardless of background—or they must abandon the American dream that education is, or should be, an instrument to ensure the opportunity for personal achievement in an open democratic society.

—Phillip C. Schlechty, Founder, Center
for Leadership in School Reform

Teachers have a special responsibility to convey the moral importance of cooperation to their students. Small-group methods that involve intergroup competition should be monitored closely. Competition can be fun, and insisting that it has no place whatever in cooperative arrangements leads us into unnecessary confrontation. But, if competition induces insensitive interactions, teachers should draw this to the attention of their students and suggest alternative strategies. Such discussions can lead to interesting and fruitful analyses of competition at other levels of society.

—Nel Noddings, Stanford University

Continue to give traditional grades in all courses but include a student progress report using the standards that describe levels of performance for that course. This will provide parents with a sense that the system as they knew it is still functioning. The additional student progress report will provide students and parents with highly specific and useful information about student performance on standards in each course.

—Robert J. Marzano, Cardinal
Stritch University

When someone says that schools are producing an awful work force, you can respond that study after study continues to find the U.S. worker to be the most productive in the world. . . . Blaming schools for competitiveness woes is a common way of deflecting responsibility from those who actually have something to do with competitiveness. If we were developing a generation of idiots, we most likely would not see the rising test scores and A-one

performances in international comparisons of reading that U.S. students have received.

—Gerald W. Bracey
educational researcher

Teachers who do not take their own education seriously, who do not study, who make little effort to keep abreast of events have no moral authority to coordinate the activities of the classroom.

—Paolo Freire (1921-1997), Author
Pedagogy of the Oppressed

The first idea that the child must acquire in order to be actively disciplined is that of the difference between good and evil; and the task of the educator lies in seeing that the child does not confound good with immobility, and evil with activity.

—Maria Montessori (1870-1952)
Author, *The Montessori Method*

Interdisciplinary teaching enables teachers to reinforce each other's work on common themes and shows students the connectedness of things, which deepens their understanding of complex issues, and permits better use of instructional time. We need to replace the "great American endurance test" with performance-based learning.

—Gordon Cawelti, Educational
Research Service

At every level, experience is necessary to the development of intelligence.

—Jean Piaget (1896-1980), Author
*The Origins of Intelligence
in Children*

It is simplistic, ill-founded and irresponsible to suggest that the major reason for the misassignment of teachers is principals assigning teachers without a concern for either the teachers or the students. The realities of teacher recruitment, selection and placement force principals essentially to play the hand they are dealt.

—Gerald N. Tirozzi, Executive
Director, National Association
of Secondary School Principals

Today's effective principal constructs a shared vision with members of the school community, convenes the conversations, insists on a student learning focus, evokes and supports leadership in others, models and participates in collaborative practices, helps pose the questions, and facilitates dialogue that addresses the confounding issues of practice. This work requires skill and new understanding; it is much easier to tell or to manage than it is to perform as a collaborative instructional leader.

—Linda Lambert, California
State University, Hayward

A major flaw in our traditional educational system is that we try but consistently fail to "motivate" students to do useless work. Boss-managers can't seem to learn that there is no way to motivate people to do what has no chance of satisfying their needs. Turned off by the pain of doing so much useless work, some students even refuse to learn useful skills like writing and math.

—William Glasser, Founder
The William Glasser Institute

What we have in the Declaration [of Independence] are the seeds of democracy as an educational theory. . . . With a slight substitution of words, we have the central mission of public education: All students are created equal. They are endowed by their creator with an inalienable right to an education that will accord them life, liberty, and the pursuit of happiness.

—Carl D. Glickman, Founder
The Program for School Improvement

Teachers have long known—and often complained—that their responsibilities seldom change from the first to the last day of work. For most, the routines of planning, teaching, grading, and meeting recur with little variation through the years. In the end, it is memorable students rather than professional milestones that highlight the phases of a typical career in teaching.

—Susan Moore Johnson
Harvard University

If IQ rules, it is only because we let it. And when we let it rule, we choose a bad master. We got ourselves into this test mess; we can get ourselves out of it.

—Robert J. Sternberg
Yale University

If tests could be composed of tasks that we value—essays, hands-on science tests—then the very act of preparing for the test would be educationally sound.

—Grant P. Wiggins, Co-founder
Center on Learning, Assessment
and School Structure

Effective teachers manage. Ineffective teachers discipline. You manage a store. You don't discipline a store. You manage a team. You don't discipline a team. You don't discipline a class. You manage a class. If there are no procedures, how do you have responsibility?

—Harry Wong
educational consultant

The classroom itself, where students come face to face with others who are different from themselves, is the place for real integration. When they are in the same classroom, all students can take advantage of the benefits and instructional expertise that may have

been reserved previously for "upper-track" (that is, white middle-class) students.

—Gloria Ladson-Billings, University
of Wisconsin

In organizations, goals erode because of low tolerance for emotional tension. Nobody wants to be the messenger with bad news. The easiest path is to just pretend there is no bad news, or better yet, "declare victory"—to redefine the bad news as not so bad by lowering the standard against which it is judged. The dynamics of emotional tension exist at all levels of human activity. They are the dynamics of compromise, the path of mediocrity. As Somerset Maugham said, "Only mediocre people are always at their best." . . . Truly creative people use the gap between vision and current reality to generate energy for change.

—Peter M. Senge, Massachusetts
Institute of Technology

Reformers have frequently ignored the enabling conditions necessary for educators to lead, thereby smothering rather than nourishing classroom, school, and district leadership.

—Larry Cuban, Stanford University

Schools in the USA (and perhaps other nations) are the scapegoat for economic ills, but are not viewed as the source of economic success. They are viewed as perpetual underperformers that need to

be constantly goaded and threatened, regardless of economic conditions.

—Henry M. Levin
Stanford University

Society exists through a process of transmission quite as much as biological life. This transmission occurs by means of communication of habits of doing, thinking, and feeling from the older to the younger. Without this communication of ideals, hopes, expectations, standards, opinions, from those members of society who are passing out of the group life to those who are coming into it, social life could not survive.

—John Dewey (1859-1952), Author
Democracy and Education

Schools face not only a crisis of public confidence but, more dangerous, a crisis of self-confidence. Not only can we no longer expect that citizens without school-age children will support education, we can no longer assume that people with school-age children will offer up their progeny and patronage. Even worse, we can no longer take for granted that those who staff our public schools believe that they are engaged in a vital cause.

—Roland S. Barth, Founder
Harvard Principal Center

Performance, of course, means the ability to do something; it is active and creative. Recognizing a correct answer out of a

predetermined list of responses is fundamentally different from the act of reading, or writing, or speaking, or reasoning, or dancing, or anything else that human beings do in the real world.

—Linda Darling-Hammond
Stanford University

We believe that we can solve the problems of crime by reopening the doors to the gas chamber and by building more prisons. But it's never been that simple. Nor is solving the problems of schooling as simple as having national education standards. And so I believe that we must invite our communities to join us in a conversation that deepens our understanding of the educational process and advances our appreciation of its possibilities. Genuine education reform is not about shallow efforts that inevitably fade into oblivion. It is about vision, conversation, and action designed to create a genuine and evolving educational culture.

—Elliot W. Eisner
Stanford University

Only if we expand and reformulate our view of what counts as human intellect will we be able to devise more appropriate ways of assessing it and more effective ways of educating it.

—Howard Gardner
Harvard University

The correct purpose of a school of education is . . . the professional one. A school of education not producing teachers is an anomaly that provokes mischief.

—John I. Goodlad, Center for
Educational Renewal, University
of Washington

The self-esteem movement is only the latest version of a familiar American emphasis on positive thinking and self-help—a tradition that has long served the interests of those who benefit from the status quo. Nothing maintains the current arrangement of power more effectively than an approach that ignores the current arrangement of power—and that focuses attention instead on how you feel about yourself.

—Alfie Kohn, educational theorist

The business of schools is to develop activities and work assignments that attract and engage students and that sustain and motivate them over time. The work that students are assigned or encouraged to undertake must have qualities that respond to the needs and values students bring to the task, just as businesses must produce products that conform with the requirements of their customers. Like profit, learning will occur if schools do their business right. Schools cannot do without learning, for those who invest in schools and those who support them will withdraw their support if learning does not occur.

—Phillip C. Schlechty, Founder, Center
for Leadership in School Reform

When the community trusts the school, it will be willing to listen, support, forgive and understand. If there is a crisis, the community's reactions will depend on the relationship that the school and community have built in the past. Building this kind of trust is a long, continuous process, not one fancy meeting.

—Dennis Littky, Founder
The Big Picture Company

When someone says teachers ought to be held accountable for their pupils' test scores, you can say that you agree, but only if certain conditions are met: (1) the accountability must factor in what the child brings to the classroom (John Locke notwithstanding, no child is a tabula rasa); (2) the test must reflect what is being taught in the classroom; (3) the focus must be on changes in test scores, not levels of test scores (the level of achievement is powerfully affected by family and community variables not under the school's control); and (4) the test must not narrow the curriculum.

—Gerald W. Bracey
educational researcher

This is the road I have tried to follow as a teacher: living my convictions; being open to the process of knowing and sensitive to the experience of teaching as an art; being pushed forward by the challenges that prevent me from bureaucratizing my practice; accepting my limitations, yet always conscious of the necessary effort to overcome them and aware that I cannot hide them because to do so would be a failure to respect both my students and myself as a teacher.

—Paolo Freire (1921-1997), Author
Pedagogy of the Oppressed

The first essential step towards reading and writing success is to have good preschool experiences available to all children. This would ensure that almost all children entered school easily able to converse with others about the world and how they understood it.

—Marie M. Clay, Founder
Reading Recovery

Principals are middle managers. As such, they face a classical organizational dilemma. Rapport with teachers is critical as is satisfying those in the hierarchy. The endless supply of new policies, programs and procedures ensures that this dilemma remains active. The expectation that principals should be the leaders in the implementation of changes which they have had no hand in developing and may not understand is especially troublesome.

—Michael Fullan, Ontario Institute
for Studies in Education, University
of Toronto

As long as improvement is dependent on a single person or a few people or outside directions and forces, it will fail. Schools, and the people in them, have a tendency to depend too much on a strong principal or other authority for direction and guidance.

—Linda Lambert, California
State University, Hayward

The right to education . . . is neither more nor less than the right of an individual to develop normally, in accord with all the potential he possesses, and the obligation that society has to transform this potential into useful and effective fulfillment.

—Jean Piaget (1896-1980), Author
The Origins of Intelligence in Children

In a traditional school, it does not even cross children's minds that they own anything; to them everything is owned by the staff and the school. We all know that what we don't own and what we have no control over acquiring has much less chance to be seen by any of us as quality than something that is ours. In a quality school, the goal would be to tell students that this is their school and involve them in as many decisions about school as you can.

—William Glasser, Founder
The William Glasser Institute

We have not understood that for democracy to work, it must be viewed as a way of learning as much as a way of governing. The disconnection of democracy from how we educate our young has led to a lack among our citizenry of the competence, skills, and understanding necessary to live, learn, and work in and for a democratic society.

—Carl D. Glickman, Founder
The Program for School Improvement

Public schools can attract and retain skilled, knowledgeable, and committed teachers only if they compensate them well and support

them in their work. In the current debate about the quality of new teachers, some would say that setting high standards is all that matters. But this strategy can work only if there is a long line of able candidates seeking to enter the profession. There is not. And yet school districts must, and will, hire a teacher for every classroom. Until teaching can compete with other lines of work, new entrants will be less than the best: less than what our society needs, less than our children deserve.

—Susan Moore Johnson
Harvard University

One of the biggest obstacles to the development of what I call successful intelligence is negative expectations on the part of authority figures. When these authority figures, whether they are teachers, administrators, parents, or employers, have low expectations, it often leads to their getting from an individual what they expect. The process may start in school, but it usually doesn't end there. Low grades become a ticket to life's slow lane. Thus, it's not a low IQ per se that can so easily lead us down the road to ruin; it's the negative expectations that are generated.

—Robert J. Sternberg, Yale University

Give students a test that's engaging, bracing, challenging and they rise to the occasion and I would argue that that has got to be a more valid measure of their achievement.

—Grant P. Wiggins, Co-founder
Center on Learning
Assessment and School Structure

In an effective classroom students should not only know what they are doing, they should also know why and how.

—Harry Wong, educational consultant

Colleagueship does not mean that you need to agree or share the same views. On the contrary, the real power of seeing each other as colleagues comes into play when there are differences of view. It is easy to feel collegial when everyone agrees. When there are significant disagreements, it is more difficult. But the payoff is also much greater. Choosing to view "adversaries" as "colleagues with different views" has the greatest benefits.

—Peter M. Senge, Massachusetts
Institute of Technology

When are we going to finally accept the idea that the future of education should not be just an extrapolation of the past? Educational practice needs to be completely redefined, and if it is not, all of our enthusiasm surrounding technology will be meaningless.

—David Thornburg, Founder
The Thornburg Center

Those who tear down are a dime a dozen; those who build are scarce. It is important to have leaders with vision and who can say what is right rather than just what is wrong. Many of us become so consumed with gaining power that we forget what we wanted to

do with it. Good social-change agents must try not just to point out what is wrong but to offer constructive alternatives for what can be tried instead, constantly adjusting the menu of alternatives to changing needs and politics.

—Marian Wright Edelman, Founder
Children's Defense Fund

Abraham Lincoln once said, "He has the right to criticize who has the heart to help." So today I say to the critics of public education: When you see something wrong, have the heart to help. But if you don't have the heart, please just get out of the way and let the rest of us get on with the job of improving our schools.

—Richard W. Riley, former
U.S. Secretary of Education

Institutions reform slowly, and as long as we wait, depending on "them" to do the job for us—forgetting that institutions are also "us"—we merely postpone reform and continue the slow slide into cynicism that characterizes too many teaching careers. There is an alternative to waiting: we can reclaim our belief in the power of inwardness to transform our work and our lives. We became teachers because we once believed that ideas and insight are at least as real and powerful as the world that surrounds us. Now we must remind ourselves that inner reality can give us leverage in the realm of objects and events.

—Parker J. Palmer, Founder, Fetzer
Institute Teacher Formation Program

Suggested Reading

Barth, R. S. (1990). *Improving schools from within: Teachers, parents, and principals can make the difference.* San Francisco: Jossey-Bass.

Bloom, B. S. (1981). *All our children learning: A primer for parents, teachers, and other educators.* New York: McGraw-Hill.

Bolman, L. G., & Deal, T. L. (1994). *Becoming a teacher leader: From isolation to collaboration.* Thousand Oaks, CA: Corwin.

Bourdieu, P. (1996). *The state nobility: Elite schools in the field of power.* Stanford, CA: Stanford University Press.

Cawelti, G. (Ed.). (1999). *Handbook of research on improving student achievement.* Arlington, VA: Educational Research Service.

Chomsky, N. (2000). *Chomsky on mis-education.* Lanham, MD: Rowman & Littlefield.

Clay, M. (1994). *Reading recovery: A guidebook for teachers in training.* Portsmouth, NH: Heinemann.

Cuban, L. (1988). *The managerial imperative and the practice of leadership in schools.* Albany: State University of New York Press.

Darling-Hammond, L. (1997). *The right to learn: A blueprint for creating schools that work.* San Francisco: Jossey-Bass

Dewey, J. (1916). *Democracy and education.* New York: Macmillan.

Dryfoos, J. G. (1994). *Full-service schools: A revolution in health and social services for children, youth, and families.* San Francisco: Jossey-Bass.

Du Bois, W. E. B. (1973). *The education of black people; ten critiques, 1906–1960.* Amherst: University of Massachusetts Press.

Edelman, M. W. (1987). *Families in peril: An agenda for social change.* Cambridge, MA: Harvard University Press.

Eisner, E. W. (1994). *The educational imagination: On the design and evaluation of school programs.* New York: Macmillan.

Freire, P. (1971). *Pedagogy of the oppressed.* New York: Seabury.

Gardner, H. (1983). *Frames of mind: The theory of multiple intelligences.* New York: Basic Books.

Fuhrman, S. (Ed.). (2001). *From the capitol to the classroom: Standards-based reform in the states.* Chicago: University of Chicago Press.

Fullan, M. (2001). *Leading in a culture of change.* San Francisco: Jossey-Bass.

Glasser, W. (1986). *Control theory in the classroom.* New York: Perennial Library.

Glickman, C. D. (1998). *Revolutionizing America's schools.* San Francisco: Jossey-Bass.

Goodlad, J. I. (1994). *Educational renewal: Better teachers, better schools.* San Francisco: Jossey-Bass.

Guilford, J. P. (1968). *Intelligence, creativity, and their educational implications.* San Diego, CA: R. R. Knapp.

Hargreaves, A. (1994). *Changing teachers, changing times: Teachers' work and culture in the postmodern age.* New York: Teachers College Press.

Johnson, S. M. (1996). *Leading to change: The challenge of the new superintendency.* San Francisco: Jossey-Bass.

Kohn, A. (2000). *The case against standardized testing: Raising the scores, ruining the schools.* Portsmouth, NH: Heinemann.

Kozol, J. (1991). *Savage inequalities: Children in America's schools.* New York: Crown.

Ladson-Billings, G. (1994). *The dreamkeepers: Successful teachers of African American children.* San Francisco: Jossey-Bass.

Lambert, L. (1998). *Building leadership capacity in schools.* Alexandria, VA: Association for Supervision and Curriculum Development.

Levin, H. M. (1983). *Cost-effectiveness: A primer.* Beverly Hills, CA: Sage.

Lieberman, A. (Ed.). (1988). *Building a professional culture in schools.* New York: Teachers College Press.

Marzano, R. J. (1992). *A different kind of classroom: Teaching with dimensions of learning.* Alexandria, VA: Association for Supervision and Curriculum Development.

Montessori, M. (1912). *The Montessori method.* New York: Frederick A. Stokes.

Noddings, N. (1992). *The challenge to care in schools: An alternative approach to education.* New York: Teachers College Press.

Odden, A., & Picus, L. O. (1992). *School finance: A policy perspective.* New York: McGraw-Hill.

Palmer, P. J. (1998). *The courage to teach: Exploring the inner landscape of a teacher's life.* San Francisco: Jossey-Bass.

Piaget, J. (1953). *Origins of intelligence in the child.* London: Routledge & Kegan Paul.

Postman, N. (1995). *The end of education: Redefining the value of school.* New York: Knopf.

Sarason, S. B. (1998). *Charter schools: Another flawed educational reform?* New York: Teachers College Press.

Schlechty, P. C. (1997). *Inventing better schools: An action plan for educational reform.* San Francisco: Jossey-Bass.

Senge, P. M. (1990). *The fifth discipline: The art and practice of the learning organization.* Garden City, NY: Doubleday.

Sergiovanni, T. J. (1994). *Building community in schools.* San Francisco: Jossey-Bass.

Sizer, T. R. (1984). *Horace's compromise: The dilemma of the American high school.* Boston: Houghton Mifflin.

Sternberg, R. J. (1990). *Metaphors of mind: Conceptions of the nature of intelligence.* New York: Cambridge University Press.

Thornburg, D. D. (1994). *Education in the communication age.* San Carlos, CA: D.D. Thornburg and Starsong.

Tomlinson, C. A. (1999). *The differentiated classroom: Responding to the needs of all learners.* Alexandria, VA: Association for Supervision and Curriculum Development.

Tyack, D. B. (1974). *The one best system: A history of American urban education.* Cambridge, MA: Harvard University Press.

Tyler, R. W. (1949). *Basic principles of curriculum and instruction.* Chicago: University of Chicago Press.

Vygotsky, L. S. (1964). *Thought and language.* Cambridge: MIT Press.

Wiggins, G. P. (1993). *Assessing student performance: Exploring the purpose and limits of testing.* San Francisco: Jossey-Bass.

Wong, H. K. & Wong, R. (2001). *The first days of school: How to be an effective teacher.* Mountain View, CA: Harry K. Wong Publications.

Author Index

Barth, Roland S., 2, 14, 24, 34, 46, 55, 66, 77, 87, 95, 104, 114, 124, 133

Bloom, Benjamin S., 17, 133

Bolman, Lee G., 21, 30, 40, 52, 61, 82, 92, 110, 133

Bourdieu, Pierre, 7, 108, 133

Bracey, Gerald W., 6, 12, 37, 49, 59, 70, 80, 86, 90, 107, 119, 127

Carter, Gene R., 40, 72, 92

Cawelti, Gordon, 38, 59, 81, 99, 119, 133

Cervantes, Miguel de, 1

Chomsky, Noam, 7, 27, 133

Clay, Marie M., 9, 19, 28, 50, 70, 90, 108, 128, 133

Cuban, Larry, 2, 12, 24, 33, 46, 51, 65, 76, 86, 95, 104, 114, 123, 133

Darling-Hammond, Linda, 3, 14, 24, 35, 46, 56, 66, 77, 87, 96, 102, 115, 125, 133

Deal, Terrence E., 100, 133

Dewey, John, 1, 13, 23, 33, 45, 55, 65, 76, 85, 95, 104, 115, 124, 133

Dryfoos, Joy G., 75, 85, 94, 133

Du Bois, W.E.B., 11, 74, 94, 113, 133

Edelman, Marian Wright, 11, 32, 54, 132, 133

Eisner, Elliot W., 2, 8, 16, 25, 34, 47, 56, 68, 78, 87, 96, 115, 125, 133

Ferrandino, Vincent L., 70, 106

Freire, Paulo, 18, 27, 34, 38, 49, 73, 80, 90, 98, 107, 119, 127, 133

Fuhrman, Susan H., 67, 134

Fullan, Michael, 8, 28, 50, 71, 91, 108, 128, 134

Gardner, Howard, 3, 16, 25, 35, 47, 57, 68, 78, 88, 97, 105, 116, 125, 133

Glasser, William, 10, 20, 30, 41, 52, 61, 72, 82, 121, 129, 134

Glickman, Carl D., 6, 31, 53, 73, 93, 101, 111, 121, 129, 134

Goodlad, John I., 4, 16, 25, 39, 47, 68, 78, 88, 97, 105, 111, 116, 126, 134

Guilford, J.P., 22, 42, 63, 84, 103, 134

Hargreaves, Andy, 45, 65, 76, 85, 95, 134

Houston, Paul D., 23, 49, 89, 103

Johnson, Susan Moore, 10, 21, 41, 62, 83, 93, 101, 110, 121, 130, 134

Kohn, Alfie, 4, 17, 26, 36, 48, 57, 67, 79, 89, 98, 106, 117, 126, 134

Kozol, Jonathan, 12, 18, 43, 64, 84, 113, 134

Ladson-Billings, Gloria, 22, 42, 64, 84, 103, 123, 134

Lambert, Linda, 120, 128, 134

Levin, Henry M., 33, 44, 124, 134

Lieberman, Ann, 58, 96, 134

Littky, Dennis, 107, 127

Marzano, Robert J., 37, 79, 118, 134

Montessori, Maria, 19, 35, 59, 80, 99, 119, 134

Noddings, Nel, 5, 15, 27, 37, 48, 58, 69, 79, 86, 90, 97, 106, 118, 134

Odden, Allan, 9, 30, 52, 60, 82, 101, 134

Paige, Rod, 18, 39, 60, 73, 100, 116

Palmer, Parker J., 4, 15, 19, 26, 36, 48, 57, 69, 98, 109, 110, 117, 132, 134

Piaget, Jean, 9, 19, 39, 60, 81, 99, 120, 129, 1314

Picus, L. O., 134

Postman, Neil, 13, 55, 134

Riley, Richard W., 29, 51, 72, 91, 109, 132

Sarason, Seymour B., 21, 41, 45, 62, 66, 74, 83, 93, 102, 112, 135

Schlechty, Phillip C., 5, 17, 26, 38, 44, 58, 69, 79, 89, 98, 106, 117, 126, 135

Senge, Peter M., 23, 123, 131, 135

Sergiovanni, Thomas J., 32, 54, 75, 111, 135

Sizer, Theodore R., 3, 7, 15, 22, 28, 36, 44, 56, 67, 77, 88, 105, 114, 135

Sternberg, Robert J., 11, 22, 31, 42, 53, 122, 130, 135

Thornburg, David, 1, 20, 29, 51, 72, 92, 109, 131, 135

Tirozzi, Gerald N., 20, 40, 61, 81, 100, 120

Tomlinson, Carol A., 14, 87, 113, 135

Tyack, David B., 13, 32, 43, 54, 64, 135

Tyler, Ralph W., 5, 135

Vygotsky, L. S., 8, 29, 50, 71, 97, 108, 135

Wiggins, Grant P., 63, 74, 83, 94, 102, 112, 130, 135

Wong, Harry, 10, 31, 53, 77, 94, 112, 122, 131, 135

Wong, Rosemary, 10, 31, 53, 135

**CORWIN
PRESS**

The Corwin Press logo—a raven striding across an open book—represents the union of courage and learning. Corwin Press is committed to improving education for all learners by publishing books and other professional development resources for those serving the field of K–12 education. By providing practical, hands-on materials, Corwin Press continues to carry out the promise of its motto: "**Helping Educators Do Their Work Better.**"